Lanterns of Light

Illuminating Your Way Home

Aneta Ardelian Kuzma

Lanterns of Light

Edited by George Verongos

Cover design by Isabella Kuzma

Paperback ISBN: 979-8-9874600-4-7

Digital ISBN: 979-8-9874600-5-4

Advance praise for *Lanterns of Light*

I read the first chapter ("The Seed of Faith") of Aneta's book, and it was perfectly timed (maybe even divine timing) for where I'm at in my life. I initially wanted to be an early reader because Aneta and I met back in November of 2023, and I have always admired the way she stepped away from corporate (as a former leader in corporate as well), built her business, and continues to help others do the same. However, I didn't know she was led so fiercely in faith. Finding Aneta and then reading the first chapter of this book...it helped me reconnect with my faith in a time when I needed a gentle reminder. I felt connected to Aneta and her message in particular when I read, "I was desperately trying to think my way to answers, listening to the loud voices in my head instead of the gentle whisper of my soul. The world's constant noise was drowning out both God's voice and my own intuition."

~Jenna Rogers

What you write is soul-stirring. It awakens the senses. In the world we are in, where there is an overwhelming sense that unless you subscribe to a militant, exclusive, dogmatic belief in God's Word that is patriarchal, exclusionary, and damning, you are somehow broken, flawed, and unworthy. Your words provide a counter that welcomes us in and lets us know that we have always belonged.

~Jason Rudman

HOW WONDERFUL!! I didn't know whether to SHOUT or cry! You touched on so many subjects deep within my being as a child of God, a pastor's kid, and raised in a family where THIS stuff you wrote about IS the reason I am who I am and have what I have today. It's the choice of choosing to believe in God, this higher power we define as such. It's a lifelong, constant conversation or relationship with an unknown entity, and the miraculous stories we CHOOSE to believe in that define spirituality.

~Alvin McCray

This chapter ("Chapter 19: The Light for Your Path") was a gentle yet powerful reminder that we don't need the whole map to move forward—only the step God has illuminated for us today. It left me feeling encouraged, peaceful, and more willing to trust in His timing. Aneta, you are a true inspiration, showing all of us how walking by faith and trusting His wisdom can transform a life. Thank you for sharing your journey so openly and beautifully.

~Laura Friscan

I have been a follower of Jesus most of my life. I grew up going to church and learning about the Bible. But it took me a while to develop a true relationship with Jesus. That is why "The Greatest Commandment," resonated with me. Love the Lord with all my heart, soul, strength, and mind, and my neighbor as myself. This commandment from Jesus makes it sound so simple, but as Aneta says, it is one of the hardest to implement. As I read this chapter, I was reminded that Jesus is at the center of everything I do. Aneta helped me see that if Jesus is truly at the center of my life, then every decision I make, idea I have, person I encounter will be a testament to "The Greatest Commandment" given. As you read this book, these God-breathed words will stir a deeper faith within you, drawing you closer into a relationship with God.

~Dorina Kramer

Aneta is a long-time friend, and reading her book feels like having a one-on-one in-person conversation with her! Her writing is honest, calming, encouraging, and thought-provoking. She can take a complicated topic and deliver it in a way that is easily understood. With her suggested practices, you are guided through things that you may not have been able or willing to sort through on your own.

~Jennifer Dietz

While Aneta's first book, *Live the Width of Your Life*, focused on the motivation to change, this book focuses on the belief in oneself to allow change. Desire and motivation are important, but without faith in one's ability, change is difficult. In this book, Aneta shows how faith and belief foster confidence, freedom, and trust, which in turn allow the release of fear, worry, and judgment, as well as genuine growth. For anyone seeking a true path to change, look no further than this book.

~Alison Muller

I have a notebook full of scribbles of profound thoughts shared by my friend (Aneta) over the course of many years. She has now gracefully composed a collection of these observations for all to read. This book is a thoughtful connection that gives the reader encouragement and permission to follow their heart, and trust that God has a purposeful plan for everyone...if only you let go, work in tandem with His voice, and have faith. Enjoy the read and where it takes you!

~Camie Miller

Thank you for sharing. "God's Ways Are Higher" reminded me to go to God with everything—gratitude, hopes, needs, and then create space to listen. The exercises in "Abundant Life Practices" are reminders to think about how your life could look and taking that to God. I should involve God in my dreams more and not just asking for help when things are difficult for myself or loved ones. I am always thankful, but talking to God in the planning stages is something I need to focus on. I like that you have separate sections for the Bible verse, personal application, journal prompt, and exercise. I can see readers going to chapters that reflect where they are at certain points in their lives, reflecting on the verse, and completing the exercises. When studying a book of the Bible, I always learn ways to apply the lessons to my life. *Lanterns of Light* can work the same way by going to a chapter that meets you where you are in life, providing a spiritual reference and practical application.

~Ronna Cunningham

This book absolutely spoke to my soul!

As someone who gets caught up in the daily grind and forgets the bigger picture, this was exactly what I needed to read. Aneta's message about remembering our inner divinity and connection to God hit me right in the heart.

What resonated most was the reminder that we become unkind when we forget we are unconditionally loved and disconnect from the fruits of the Spirit—love, joy, peace, patience, kindness, goodness, faithfulness, gentleness, and self-control. It's so true! When I'm frustrated or stuck in worry and fear, I close off and lose that lightness. This book gently pulled me back to what matters most.

The concept of "leading with LOVE" has become my daily mantra since reading this. It's a simple but powerful reminder that my life is meant for something so much bigger than sitting in anxiety and self-doubt.

I also loved the practical elements—especially the "date with the divine" practice Aneta shared. It sparked something new that I've now added to my morning routine, and it's already transforming how I start my days.

This book feels like a loving conversation with a wise friend who reminds you of your true worth and purpose. If you're a high achiever who sometimes forgets that you're here to do meaningful work in the world, this is a must-read.

Thank you, Aneta, for sharing your wisdom and heart with the world. I feel honored to have received this energy, love, and insight!

Highly recommend for anyone ready to remember their divine purpose and lead with love.

~Samantha Lane

What struck me most was the theme in "Chapter 12: God's Handiwork" centered around the powerful reminder that God doesn't wait for the qualified—He qualifies the called. The message that truly stayed with me is that God consistently uses the unlikely, the unprepared, and the seemingly unfit to carry out His work. It's not about our qualifications or our confidence; it's about our willingness. Through every story and reflection, this chapter emphasizes that the equipping, the preparation, the courage to say "yes"...they all come from God. The Holy Spirit steps in, intercedes, and fills in the gaps we can't. For anyone who's ever felt inadequate or questioned their worth in God's plan, this book is a wake-up call; a deeply personal reminder that it's not our strength He needs, but our surrender.

~Maeghan Gorman

Within one week, I was given several signs about mustard seed faith—including my husband being gifted a literal mustard seed in a vial by a woman he had just met. When Aneta said, "God is chasing you, Aimee," and shared this chapter ("Chapter 2: Faith That Moves Mountains") with me, I knew she was right. Reading it brought me back to the hardest moments of my life—the ones where my faith was tested with huge crosses to bear. What I did have was prayer. A deep, desperate asking. And that tiny seed of faith—paired with a willing heart—was enough for God to not only move mountains, but to bless me with miracles.

This chapter reminded me that we don't need to be perfect to be loved. We don't need unwavering belief to be heard. Aneta has a gift for making faith feel safe, warm, and welcoming. Her words have invited me to return to God in a way that feels deeply healing. And the embodiment exercises—so simple, yet powerful—are something I now reach for whenever I feel shaky or unsure. It brings the message out of my head and back into my body.

This chapter is an anchor. A reminder that even the smallest faith—paired with surrender—can move mountains. I find myself returning to it often, especially when I need to remember: I don't have to carry it all alone. God is here to help.

~Aimee Smith

The message from "Chapter 4: Touch of Faith" is raw and genuine, speaking to many of us on numerous occasions in our lives. It's a message that's always relevant, no matter where we are in our journey. We disconnect, unfortunately, so rapidly from our faith and belief in ourselves and GOD. We often overlook the power that we all possess when we choose to utilize it. Through our belief in ourselves and faith in God, we can move mountains and change the world, starting with our own. This potential for personal growth is a beacon of hope in our journey. This book will change many lives for the better if we apply the teachings and exercises in it.

~Adriana Bisorca

This is beautiful, Aneta, and beautifully written. "Being vs. doing" has been the theme of most of my adult spiritual life. I love your questions at the end. They are nonjudgmental and inviting. They don't prompt performance but allow reflection, letting the story and your words naturally draw out what is within the reader. I love this and can't wait to read the whole book.

~Laura Larson

What is truly helpful to me with the readings is that each time I go back to look at them, something different jumps out at me based on my current situation or mood. You provide a relatable perspective, and it always seems to be just what I need. I appreciate the action steps. I hear your voice reading to me. Your words inspire calm and contentment and remind me that I have the tools I need to make the best out of this life I'm living.

~Darla Costa

Lanterns of Light is a soulful, spirit-led journey back to who we truly are. With wisdom and warmth, Aneta weaves story, Scripture, and reflection into a guide for releasing perfectionism, embracing faith, and walking in partnership with God. Each page is a gentle nudge back into freedom, clarity, and the sacred truth that we are already "very good."

~Stephanie Van Deynze-Snell

In true divine order, I was able to read a few chapters of Aneta's book *Lanterns of Light* before she published it, and let me just say, it unlocked something deep and profoundly healing in me. As a recovering perfectionist, I had forgotten that God's unconditional love was always available, how I know I am enough and worthy, and a true healing companion. The way Aneta writes speaks directly to my soul and brought me to tears. Tears in celebration of this beautiful remembering that I am being called home. Home to myself. Home to God. Home to Spirit. And it couldn't have come at a better time. This book is a modern-day reclamation and is so needed worldwide. Aneta has a way of truth-telling that'll move you. Her style includes the Word, her reflections on it, and tangible things we can do to integrate the teachings into our lives immediately.

~Brooke Jean

As someone who has had a challenging relationship with religion and God, I was not sure how this book would land for me. I was so pleasantly surprised to feel so inspired to revisit and rekindle my relationship with God. The way Aneta so lovingly and tenderly wrote this book made me feel like she was there holding my hand as I was reading it. My biggest takeaways are that we are all created from his love and image. It was a reminder that God is not outside of but already living within me, a part of my spirit, my heart, and my essence. No matter if I stray, God will always be there waiting for me whenever I'm ready to commune with him again. This book is a must-read!

~Caroline Charlton

"Chapter 3: By Your Faith Let It Be Done," truly stirred something in me. Your reflections on faith felt like a warm reminder to trust more deeply, to surrender what I try so hard to control. The way you connected scripture, personal experience, and embodiment was powerful; it made the message not just something to read, but something to feel. Your words are a gift, and this chapter is a gentle guide back to God's presence in the everyday. Thank you for sharing your heart and truth so beautifully.

~Lucia Almeida-Oliveira

Aneta's work is truly powerful. I especially appreciate her willingness to share her personal journal entries and speak openly about her vulnerabilities. This level of honesty made the messages resonate deeply with me. What stood out most was the way she broke down familiar Bible verses. Although I've read these passages before, I've never explored them with the depth and clarity she brings. Her ability to unpack scripture and reveal its deeper meaning is a true gift. This book is not only insightful but also deeply personal and encouraging. Highly recommended for anyone seeking spiritual growth, reflection, and connection.

~Jennifer Ristic

Wow!!! I'm sincerely blown away. I felt like each sentence hit home in some kind of way. And I don't feel it's talked about enough how perfectionism really does distance us from God! I love how you touched on this. We often think it's only addictions or behaviors with a "stigma" that do this. But I always say: perfectionism is the silent killer of high achievers. Your writing flows so well. I feel like I'm right there with you as I read it. It's raw, vulnerable, and full of truth. I love the piece where you give ways to put things into practice, too. Those little exercises stick with people! Thank you so much for sharing this. I can't wait to read the entire book.

~Angelica Rizzo

Aneta is a rare gift from the divine, the potency of her words that she has poured into this book landed on my heart in such a profound way—the transmission is clear and will change you on a soul level.

~Samantha Skelly

Contents

Foreword

Lanterns of Light is a guide, a rhythm, a woven journey. May you meet it as such.

As an editor, I've learned to listen not only to the words but also to the spaces between them—the rhythm, the breath, the unspoken intentions. From my first read through of *Lanterns of Light*, it was clear that this book was not just meant to be read—it was meant to be companioned.

What sets this book apart from others in the personal transformation genre is its nonlinear accessibility. You can start at the beginning and follow the journey all the way through, or you can open to any page and get exactly what you need. This design was on purpose. Aneta's structure mirrors the inner journey itself: spiraling, revisiting, unfolding—not in a straight line, but in ever-deepening layers.

Aneta has structured *Lanterns of Light* with deep care and intentionality. Each chapter stands as a self-contained lantern, unique in tone yet harmonically connected to the whole. Whether she's guiding the reader through rituals of grounding, reflections on inner peace, or stories of transformation, every section is precisely placed—not just for flow, but for resonance.

The pacing of Aneta's writing creates room for reflection, never crowding insight with excess. Her voice is gentle, yet grounded. Clear, yet warm. In a genre saturated with oversimplifications and prescriptions, she offers presence instead of pretense.

And yet, *Lanterns of Light* is more than just its architecture. As I worked with Aneta on this manuscript, it became clear that we weren't simply editing chapters—we were creating space, keeping the channel open for something subtle and luminous to emerge. The pages began to feel like vessels for frequency, each one tuned to a truth just beyond language. Her words don't seek to impress. They invite. They remember. They bring you back to yourself.

There's something rare about this book: it doesn't tell you where to go—it honors where you already are. It doesn't ask you to follow—it invites you to listen. And in doing so, it reflects one of the quiet miracles of Aneta's work: her ability to speak not *at* the reader, but *with* them; with their soul.

This book is not a spotlight. It is a lantern. Subtle, enduring, quietly radiant.

George Verongos
Editor
www.LiteraryServices.net
Ocean Shores, Washington
August 31, 2025

Introduction

I never planned to write this book. Actually, I told God "no."

Maybe you've done the same—felt a nudge in your spirit, a call you didn't think you were ready for, and pushed it away. That's where this story begins: with resistance, fear, and a God who kept pursuing me.

On November 3, 2023, during my morning meditation, I felt a powerful wave of God's unconditional love. Along with it, I received a message I couldn't ignore:

"Write a book using your favorite Bible verses as the inspiration for each chapter. Share how they've carried you. Others need to be reminded that they can come home to Me."

How many times have I asked God to use me? How often have I prayed to be a vessel for His love and wisdom? Yet when the answer came that morning, I hesitated, questioned, and resisted.

I convinced myself I wasn't the right person to write this book. What if I'm judged? What if my faith and knowledge about God's Word aren't strong enough?

Yet, God kept pursuing me. And slowly, I learned that when He whispers to the heart, He also lights our path, one step at a time.

This wasn't the book I ever imagined writing. It was a divine invitation I finally accepted, even though I was scared. And when I said "yes," something shifted. My faith deepened. My connection to God grew stronger.

Looking back, I can see how God had been preparing me all along. In 2019, during another meditation, the phrase "Lanterns of Light" came to me. I was reminded of one of my favorite verses: *"Your word is a lamp to my feet and a light to my path"* (Psalm 119:105). At the time, I didn't understand its meaning, but I journaled about it that morning. Now I see that it was the seed of this book. Our entire path is never fully lit, but we are given enough light for today.

One month before the publication of this book, I was in Morocco hosting a retreat. On the night we went to the desert, I walked into the space and saw lanterns lined up. I felt God winking at me, and reminding me that I was on the right path.

Lanterns of Light is my testimony to the living, breathing Word of God. When I was lost, these verses became lanterns of light, illuminating my path when I couldn't see the way forward.

I don't consider myself more qualified than anyone else to write this book. Like many, I've experienced fear, grief, burnout, and renewal, and found peace through God's Word. But God reminded me during this journey that I don't need to be the only one writing it, because if I let Him guide me and share what He reveals, I will have fulfilled my part.

Whether you're spiritually curious, returning to faith, or simply seeking deeper meaning, my prayer is that this book meets you where you are, and you feel less alone. May the verses illuminate not just your understanding but also your heart. I pray they guide you back home to yourself and to the God who has been waiting for you all along.

So how did this divine nudge become the book you are holding?

Each chapter begins with a verse that is meaningful to me. I share my personal thoughts and experiences, along with journal entries that reveal my most vulnerable moments. I've included these because I believe in the power of shared human experiences. When we see ourselves in each other's stories, it reminds us that we're not alone.

I'm not a theologian, pastor, or academic. I am a seeker on a spiritual journey of remembrance in this earthly body, relying on my Creator and Savior for guidance and daily alignment. This book reflects my journey of living my faith by trusting and depending on His strength and wisdom, rather than relying on my own.

Each chapter ends with prompts and practices to help you explore what His Word means in your life. I don't want you to just read this book; I want you to live it.

When we live from a place of spiritual alignment, something transformative happens. We don't just receive light—we become light. In a world filled with darkness, division, and despair, our authenticity and faith shine like lanterns in the night, guiding others toward hope, purpose, and a deeper connection with the divine.

Your Journey Starts Here

So come as you are. Bring your questions, doubts, wounds, and hopes. Let's walk this path together, guided by these lanterns of light.

What if a deeper sense of purpose, the authentic connection to something greater than yourself, is waiting for you in the pages ahead? What if the light you need for your next step is already divinely here, ready to illuminate not just where you're going, but who you are becoming?

Let's take the first step together.

With love and gratitude,

Aneta

Section 1

FAITH FOUNDATIONS

Chapter 1

The Seed of Faith

"Now faith is the assurance of things hoped for,
the conviction of things not seen." –Hebrews 11:1

Throughout most of my life, I rarely questioned my faith. I have always believed in a higher power; I trust that a loving Creator made the universe and me in His image. I believe God is a source of unconditional love, and that you and I are here for a purpose. Yet sometimes, my faith wavered when I didn't see evidence that life would unfold as I hoped. I chose this verse as the opening quote for this book because it's short, simple, and powerful, yet I find it difficult to embody it consistently in my own life. When things don't go as planned, our faith is tested.

I am grateful that Scripture has existed for thousands of years. In the stories of the Old and New Testaments, I find evidence that I am not the first to feel this way, which brings me comfort. It reminds me that the human experience is universal, and that others have also struggled with doubt, questioned their faith and purpose, and found that trusting in what we cannot see is challenging.

Understanding Authentic Faith

This verse from the New Testament is attributed to Paul, who was speaking to the early Christians and trying to offer them hope during their personal struggles. At that time, they faced persecution and uncertainty, which must have frightened them for their safety.

In this verse, the words "assurance" and "conviction" stand out to me because they are such powerful words. They describe a deep understanding that goes beyond doubt. To have this kind of certainty and spiritual clarity means we can face life's uncertainties with a steadiness that comes from trusting in what we cannot yet see and having confidence in what will happen in the future.

I try to imagine what life was like for the early believers thirty to sixty years after Jesus's death and resurrection. They were mostly a grassroots movement, following teachings that directly challenged both religious and government authorities. Many gathered in secret, risking everything for their beliefs. And remember, Jesus was no longer physically with them, and most had never even met Him in person. It's one thing to have faith when everything is going well. It's entirely different when we face challenges with no clear way out.

My deepest spiritual growth hasn't come from mountain-top moments but from the valleys, during times when I stubbornly tried to handle everything myself, only to realize I wasn't equipped. The breakthroughs occurred after I struggled alone and finally remembered that I don't have to face life on my own. In those moments of surrender, when I finally let God in and asked for help, everything changed.

Faith as Foundation

Faith is the essential first step in our spiritual journey. It's the foundation on which everything else is built. Without it, we can't please God or fully experience what He has for us.

This journey of faith isn't about having perfect understanding or never doubting. It's about choosing to trust even when the path isn't clear, even when circumstances seem to go against God's promises, and even when our feelings fluctuate.

What I've learned is that faith isn't static—it's constantly evolving and changing. Sometimes it feels strong, and other times it feels as fragile as glass, but what matters is that we hold on to it, taking small steps forward on our journey.

When we embrace faith as our foundation, everything else in our spiritual life flows naturally from this source. Our prayer life, our service to others, our ability to surrender control—all of these are expressions of the foundational faith we've established.

The beauty of faith lies in the fact that it doesn't require us to have all the answers. It simply asks us to trust the One who does. In a world obsessed with certainty and proof, faith offers a different way—a way of hope, conviction in unseen things, and assurance in God's promises, regardless of our current circumstances.

From Desert Wandering to Promised Land

I am so thankful I have been documenting my journey, because it's easy to forget my own thoughts or struggles once I've reached the other side.

Journal Entry, September 19, 2017

2017 was a year of new beginnings and fresh adventures for me. I decided to make changes in my life that would allow me to pursue some passions and goals I'd been postponing. I became a certified yoga teacher, started Reiki sessions with a close friend, launched an anonymous blog, and began writing and meditating regularly. I was also promoted at work and took on additional responsibilities. Despite enjoying these activities, I still felt very stressed and sometimes frustrated or angry.

During my morning journaling, I complained about the same issues I've struggled with for years and kept asking God to rescue me. Then, one day, I realized that my source of unhappiness was me. My thoughts and the words I spoke to myself, and others were the problem, not my circumstances. Yes, there are always situations that are challenging and less than ideal. However, the most important thing I can control is my mind, thoughts, and attitude.

My epiphany reminded me of the Old Testament story of Moses, who tried to lead his people into the Promised Land. They wandered in the desert for forty years, and many died along the way, but they never entered the Promised Land. God guided His people not in a straight line, which would have been the shortest route, but instead on the "crooked" path, out of fear that when they saw opposition, they would become afraid and want to go back to Egypt. Although they were slaves in Egypt, God feared His people would prefer slavery again rather than face the uncertainty of their new lives in an unfamiliar place. He understood that, as humans, we often choose comfort and familiarity over risk, uncertainty, and newness.

I had been wandering in the desert, praying for rescue, for years. Like the Israelites, I was more afraid of the giants in the Promised Land than confident in the size of my God. I was scared and unhappy, yet too afraid to believe God's promises for my life. One day, I realized I could enter the Promised Land at any time. And it didn't mean my circumstances had to change. It meant that I could choose to live joyfully, peacefully, and with purpose in the present moment. I could trust that the path would be clear, that I'd be supported, and that the only way to the new life I wanted for myself was to face my fears, go through challenges, and still believe.

The truth is, I always had the ability, but I kept waiting for someone or something to help me reach my goals, even though I was the one responsible for my own happiness. So, I stopped waiting, picked up my staff, and began heading toward my own Promised Land.

Faith isn't about certainty in what we see, feel, or experience. It's about believing even when we lack evidence. It's trusting without proof. When I finally understood that I could make changes in my life, I stepped into my faith without needing the whole path to be lit. That was me living my faith.

Finding Purpose in Faith

Recently, I was asked to define my "why"—why I'm a coach. The answer came easily: I want to help others who felt like I did a few years ago. I want to help women and men wake up and realize that this is it—we have one chance to live lives filled with purpose, passion, and peace. I want to help them shed limiting beliefs, rewrite the stories they tell themselves, and eliminate the excuses that hold them back from achieving what they truly desire. When we do this work, we leave our unique mark on the world by sharing our authentic talents, gifts, and experiences.

I used to lie awake at night worrying about dying young with regrets, about wasting my precious life, about running out of time to figure out what kind of life I wanted to live, and about never discovering my true dharma. I no longer carry those worries. Every day, I show up, remembering my purpose and taking aligned action. I know I am walking my path, and I've learned that the journey itself is the way.

The Journey of Faith

Life is a journey. The key question isn't whether you're on a path—we all are—but whether you know where you're headed. When you lose sight of your destination or never clearly define it, the journey becomes confusing, stagnant, and ultimately frustrating. The unavoidable challenges along the way can stop you completely if you don't have a strong "why" pulling you forward.

Looking back, I realize my biggest frustrations came from not knowing my true direction. I would have paid any price to have someone tell me where to go and what to do. But that's not how this works. No one—no mentor, teacher, or guide—can walk your path for you.

The good news is that it begins with a decision to start the journey, step onto the path, and have the courage to keep going even when it feels uncomfortable. Why? The goal is to learn how to live more fully and passionately and then share that with others. We weren't meant to live lives of mediocrity or complacency. We were created for community, connection, and greatness. Remember: wherever you are on your journey, right now is exactly where you're meant to be.

While everyone walks their own path, what we each seek varies. I believed I was pursuing my purpose, but what I was truly searching for was God's voice—that quiet whisper I couldn't hear over the noise and distractions of my past life. I was desperately trying to solve my problems by thinking my way through them, listening to the loud voices in my head instead of the gentle whisper of my soul. The constant noise of the world was drowning out both God's voice and my own intuition. I needed to slow down, pause, and listen.

I've learned that clarity rarely comes before action; it usually follows it. You don't find your way to clarity just by thinking; you find it by doing. I finally found the courage to leave behind the familiar yet unfulfilling path I was on and started moving toward something greater. Yes, there are challenges and obstacles on this new journey, but my God walks with me, and His presence gives me the strength and guidance I need. That's where I'm headed, one faithful step at a time.

Life as a Pilgrimage

For years, walking the El Camino de Santiago de Compostela has been at the top of my bucket list, especially after reading Paulo Coelho's *The Pilgrimage*. If you've never heard of it, El Camino de Santiago is an ancient pilgrimage that dates back to medieval times, with paths from all over Europe converging at the Cathedral of Santiago de Compostela in Spain. Walking "The Way," as it is often called, is a spiritual journey that has attracted pilgrims from around the world for centuries, each on their own unique journey. Pilgrims walk for weeks, carrying their belongings and the iconic scallop shell symbol. Even if someone begins the journey alone, they find community with people from various backgrounds and beliefs on the El Camino through shared meals and conversations at the many hostels along the way.

I imagined arriving at the cathedral, transformed, having found myself, my purpose, and my reason for being alive. I still hope to walk some of the trail someday, but my perspective has shifted.

I've realized that my life right now is my Camino. The path isn't on some distant Spanish road, but rather the steps I take each day, building this new life. My Camino consists of the choices I make, the fears I face, the uncertainty I navigate, and the beautiful souls I meet along the way. With each step, I see myself reflected in others, connect more deeply with God, and strengthen my faith.

As I continue walking, I release heavy burdens and stories that no longer serve me. I practice forgiving myself for past mistakes, for not "walking" more miles each day, for growing tired, and for feeling worn out when stretched beyond my comfort zone. I am reminded that this is a spiritual, emotional, mental, and physical journey.

There is a reason why El Camino is over 500 miles long and takes nearly two months to complete if you walk ten to twelve miles daily. The transformation isn't meant to happen overnight—that has never been the point. The path includes inevitable bumps, delays, injuries, and disappointments. And that's perfectly okay. I'm learning that there's no single "right way" to walk this path.

I release the expectation that I should know every detail of a journey I've never taken before. I let go of the pressure to race toward some finish line. El Camino isn't about reaching Santiago de Compostela Cathedral—it's about the journey itself. That's why it's called "The Way." Those who rush to finish, or skip parts of the path, miss the true meaning of pilgrimage. The journey, with its unexpected encounters, sudden revelations, extreme challenges, and unexpected delays, gradually chips away at our expectations, ego, and carefully crafted plans.

We don't find ourselves at the destination; we find ourselves on the path. We are refined through challenges. We learn to love ourselves as we release the old attachments and armor of protection.

Embracing Your Faith Journey

As you reflect on your faith journey, ask yourself: Is it solid? Is it growing? What steps can you take to strengthen it? Remember that even a small seed of faith can grow into something powerful when placed in God's hands.

Your Faith Practices

Faith starts as an inner certainty before it manifests externally. These practices help you find the roots of faith already within you and develop them into deliberate action. Through reflection, embodied awareness, and honest evaluation, you'll uncover where faith is prompting you to grow.

1. Journal Prompt

Where in your life do you feel called to trust even without proof? What is the "seed" of faith you are being asked to plant?

2. Embodiment Exercise

Close your eyes, take a deep breath, and imagine what it feels like to trust in something unseen fully. Feel your shoulders soften as you embrace uncertainty. That is the presence of God with you right now. Notice how your body reacts to this trust—perhaps your breathing deepens, or a sense of peace washes over you. Now, picture this seed of faith taking root inside you. With each breath, feel it grow stronger and more grounded. Do you believe that the divine is supporting you RIGHT NOW? Can you feel it? Open your eyes and write down one act of faith you can do today—one step on your journey where you'll trust without seeing the entire path.

Faith is the essential foundation of our spiritual journey and the base from which everything else grows. Although it often begins small and unseen, its impact can be deeply transformative. When faith becomes real in our lives, it can lead us to ask how we can serve, love others, and show more compassion in the world. I believe walking El Camino is powerful because of the reflective time alone with our Creator and the chance to connect with and love others who, at first, began as strangers and ultimately become family on the trail.

As we nurture this seed of faith, we realize it's not about possessing perfect understanding or unwavering confidence. It's about taking the next step forward, even when we can't see the entire path.

Will you trust today that the seed of faith already planted within you is enough to begin your journey?

Chapter 2
Faith That Moves Mountains

"Truly I tell you, if you have faith as small as a mustard seed, you can say to this mountain, 'Move from here to there', and it will move. Nothing will be impossible for you." –Matthew 17:20

I've always loved this verse and the idea that faith the size of a tiny mustard seed could move mountains. However, I don't think I've ever truly possessed such powerful faith. I understood it intellectually, but hadn't embodied it in my heart. It reminds me of when I first heard phrases like "Thoughts become things" or "It's just as easy to ask for $1M as it is to ask for $1." I nodded along, thinking I believed in these principles, but I hadn't truly integrated them into the core of who I am.

Mountains and Mustard Seeds

Jesus spoke these words to His disciples after they had tried and failed to heal a boy possessed by a demon. They were confused and discouraged, asking why they couldn't perform the healing. Jesus used this moment to talk about the power of faith and how it can move mountains. He wanted them to see that faith, even as small as a mustard seed, has enough power to overcome obstacles, bring about significant change, and accomplish what seems impossible.

Looking back at the past six years since I left my corporate career to start my own business, I realize that my decision to leap was my mustard seed moment. I had no guarantees that things would work out. In fact, I knew that if I relied just on myself, they wouldn't. The difference with this life decision was that I didn't place my faith in myself; I chose to believe in God. My confidence wasn't in my skills or experience but in the limitless God who could work through me. I had zero proof I could build a successful business, but I believed that if I aligned with God's purpose, anything was possible.

That single decision ignited one of the most profound spiritual transformations of my life. I learned to rely on God instead of myself. It involved surrendering to uncertainty and choosing trust over control. It also meant opening my heart to the truth that when we're aligned with God's purposes, nothing is truly impossible.

The Seed of Transformation

Journal Entry, February 2, 2020

I've been reflecting on this verse lately. It's a well-known Bible verse. Jesus reminds us that God has no limits. Nothing is impossible if we believe. The challenge for me is that doubt has taken up too much mental space.

The mustard seed is tiny! Yet, Jesus says that if our faith were even this small, we could command the mountains to move, and they would obey. This isn't just a powerful image but also a beautiful one. What a love story God has for us! God is urging us to ask Him for big dreams, to believe that He is limitless and wants to support us, and then to be patient and receive His blessings.

I've struggled with this my whole life. I believed in God and His power, but not always in every part of my life. I somehow felt I had to try hard and work hard, thinking I had to do it all on my own. My stubbornness and need for control kept me stuck. I journaled and begged God to show me a way out, but I often didn't follow through with what He asked. Now, I believe with every fiber of my being that God's plan for my life is so much bigger and better than I ever imagined.

So, I listen. I listen to what He tells me to do, and I follow through. Today, I am hosting a yoga session at my house for friends who wanted to try it but felt intimidated to do it at a studio. I listened when I decided to create a young adult webinar on Zoom. I believed God would guide those who needed it to the session. I built content, observed what worked, and trusted that the feedback would lead me to the next steps.

I write every day, trusting this will eventually turn into a book. It's freeing to let go of fear. It's also exciting to see the joy God brings into my life. Yes, I have proposals out there, and if I'm meant to do the work, I'd be happy to do it because I enjoy it and know I can add real value. If it doesn't happen, God will redirect me toward other things.

I will not wait or worry. I will create value every day in ways that bring me joy. I will fill myself up, care for myself, remind myself of whose child I am, and make the most of every minute of my life. I will not waste a second. I will not give in to fears, lies, or doubts. I am a walking, breathing, living miracle and will use all the good, bad, and challenging experiences to help others. Isn't that what we are all supposed to do? Isn't that what life is?

We don't know if we get to live other lives and try to do things differently. And if we do, will we remember our other lives? So, while I am here, I will do what I'm compelled to do. That feels like freedom. I feel alive. I feel hopeful and grateful for the chance to learn new things, grow, keep developing, challenge myself, and respond differently to people, drama, and noise. My intuition is on high alert. I am guided, and I can feel it at the cellular level. I am so grateful to be co-creating this BIG, BOLD, BEAUTIFUL, ABUNDANT, HEALTHY, PROSPEROUS, MULTI-PASSIONATE, PURPOSEFUL, FULFILLING LIFE with the creator of the universe. How amazing!

I don't know when the shift happened, but it has. I believe God is providing for me in many ways right now. He is meeting all my needs and wants. He is bringing the right people into my life, opening doors that were previously closed, and speaking favor over my life. He is equipping me with what I need to do His work. He is speaking directly to me. He is refining me, building my character, and removing what I no longer need. He has told us repeatedly that anything is possible. I want to be an example that this is true.

Revisiting this journal entry, rereading my words, and recalling the emotions I felt when I wrote them have renewed my faith. The power of faith isn't measured by might or strength, but by the quality of belief. When our faith is genuine, we connect with God's infinite power and resources that surpass our own. Our partnership with God enables us to move the mountains in our lives—the insurmountable challenges—that are impossible to overcome on our own.

Even the tiniest faith, like the mustard seed, has the potential to grow and expand into something greater. And when we nurture that faith and align it to God's strength, then the power of that faith is unleashed. The bigger the mountain, the bigger the miracle that God can perform through our faith.

From Small Seeds to Moved Mountains

The power of mustard seed faith isn't in its size but in what it's connected to. Even the smallest seed of faith, when anchored to our Infinite God, can achieve what seems utterly impossible.

What mountains are you facing today? What obstacles seem immovable? What situations feel completely hopeless? These are the places where even the smallest faith can demonstrate its extraordinary power.

Faith isn't about forcing ourselves to believe more through our own effort. It's about directing whatever faith we have—no matter how small—toward the God who specializes in moving mountains. When our small faith connects with His endless power, the impossible becomes possible.

There's something beautiful about God using the mustard seed as a metaphor. He could have chosen something grand or impressive, but instead, He chose one of the smallest seeds known in that culture. It's as if He's telling us, "Don't worry about how small your faith feels. That's not what matters. What matters is that you have faith at all, and that you direct it toward Me."

This has been freeing for me. For years, I felt my faith wasn't strong or large enough. I would compare myself to others who seemed to have unwavering confidence in God's promises. But Jesus's words remind me that it's not about how much faith we have, but its quality and purpose.

As you finish this chapter, identify your mountains and plant your mustard seeds. Don't wait until your faith feels bigger. Start with exactly what you have right now. The smallest step of faith today can lead to a mountain-moving transformation tomorrow.

Your Mountain-Moving Practices

Faith isn't just a concept to understand—it's a truth to embody. These practices invite you to move beyond intellectual agreement into physical, emotional, and spiritual alignment with your mustard seed faith. This is where transformation truly begins.

1. Journal Prompt

Reflect on a time in your life when you took a small action of faith, and it led to a significant transformation.

Where in your life do you feel like a mountain is standing in your way? What is one tiny step of faith you can take to begin moving it?

2. Embodiment Exercise

Stand tall, close your eyes, and imagine an obstacle or mountain in your life.

Visualize its size and what it represents, and notice what emotions come up for you.

Now, slowly take one step forward, and imagine that with each step, your faith grows bigger.

As you move forward, pause and notice how you're feeling in your body. Take a deep breath in and out, observe the obstacles melting away, and feel the possibility beginning to fill your body.

What is one step that you can take today in an act of faith?

Mountains don't move because of the size of our faith, but because of how mighty our God is. Even faith as small as a mustard seed connects us to His endless power.

The question isn't if your mountain can be moved—it can. The real miracle is that God chooses to work with our small acts of faith to achieve what seems impossible.

What small seed of faith can you plant today that could start moving your mountain tomorrow?

Chapter 3

By Your Faith Let It Be Done

"According to your faith, let it be done to you." –Matthew 9:29

Faith is a belief and trust in God, even without complete proof. This can be challenging for many of us. We often struggle to believe in a higher power, a Creator, or God, relying solely on our faith. We search for evidence of His existence, but maybe we aren't looking in the right places.

When I see a sunrise or sunset, I see God. When I breathe, I feel God moving within me. When I met my daughters for the first time, I knew they were a gift from God. When I fell in love with my husband, I thanked God. The list keeps going. I don't need scientific proof. I see God in all that is good, every single day, because I seek it.

Faith That Activates

In this verse, Jesus is approached by two blind men who ask Him to heal them so they can see. I don't know if they were blind from birth or if they had an accident, but I imagine them hearing about someone performing miracles and healing others, giving them a small bit of hope that maybe He could do the same for them. When they finally find Jesus, He asks them a powerful question: "Do you believe I can do this?"

I always find that question interesting. Their healing depends entirely on *their* faith. It's not Jesus's faith, His identity, His touch, or some mystical energy that causes the healing—it's their belief. What made their healing possible was their faith alone. The other thing I notice when reading this passage is that Jesus has them declare their belief aloud, not just silently in their minds or hearts. They declared that they believed He could heal them.

Can you imagine what it must have been like for them to see again, or for the first time? To see what they could only imagine in their mind's eye. To look upon the face of Jesus, who had made this miracle possible within them.

What must that first moment of sight have felt like? How did their lives change beyond just being able to see again after their healing? What paths did their lives take afterward, and how did their miracle spread outward to influence others? Because when we experience healing, it creates a ripple effect for everyone else who observes the miracle.

Faith as the Key

Faith is essential for receiving God's blessings and healing in our lives. I often struggle to fully trust and rely on God in every part of my life. When making important decisions—such as choosing a university, finding a job, deciding where to raise our family, handling challenges with our children, or thinking about leaving my career—I sometimes forget that God is present and ready to help. Instead, I tend to lean on my limited thoughts, changing feelings, and external opinions rather than surrendering everything to God with confidence that He is always there to support me.

Even now, I notice myself becoming stressed, running at an unsustainable pace, or distracted by unproductive thoughts. In those moments, I gently remind myself: "According to your faith, let it be done." This simple truth encourages me to release my burdens, ask for divine help, and fully trust in God.

The Power of Belief

Our faith is what unleashes God's power in our lives. Throughout Scripture, a consistent pattern emerges: Jesus first asks people if they believe, then declares that they will be healed according to their faith. Whether healing Gentiles, sinners, the demon-possessed, or those with physical disabilities, His approach was consistent: "According to your faith, let it be done to you." His question was always some variation of: "Do you believe I can do this?"

Our faith is the most powerful thing that we possess. Not our abilities. Not our intellect. Not our connections. Not our name. Not our perseverance. Our confidence should rest not in what we can do, but in what God can do through us.

And still, I find myself forgetting daily. Imposter syndrome persists because we try to rely on our own limited strength instead of God's limitless power. Jesus told His followers not to worry about what to say because God would provide the words. God doesn't call the qualified; He qualifies the called. Moses struggled with speech. David committed adultery and murder. Peter was just a fisherman with a temper. Still, God used each of them powerfully, and they stand as models of faith in scripture.

We don't need to know the details of the "how." We don't have to be perfect. We aren't the ones doing the healing—we create the conditions for healing through our beliefs. There's freedom in releasing the need to understand the how. Instead of frantically searching for answers, we can focus on one essential task: strengthening our faith, which is an internal process, and trusting that God will faithfully do His part.

Releasing Self-Reliance

This is something I need to remind myself of every day. I don't understand why I instinctively try to do things on my own. Maybe it's just how I was raised. I'm like one of my girls when they were toddlers, with hands on hips, saying, "I do it myself!" while I stood nearby, watching them struggle with something I could easily help with.

I remember when my daughters used to do this, and it would drive me crazy. Not because I wanted to take away their independence, but because I wanted to guide them and make things a little easier. Now, I find myself doing the same thing with God. I forget that there's a loving Creator just waiting to help me.

Isn't it interesting how, when someone gets sick, we immediately pray? We instinctively know we can't heal them ourselves. So, why don't we approach everything this way? Is it pride? Or do we somehow believe we're bothering God with our "little problems"? As if the Creator of the universe has more important things to worry about than us. As if we don't want to wake God up in the middle of the night with what we think are silly prayers. I don't know exactly why I do this, but I do know I'm tired of trying to figure everything out on my own.

I want to go beyond just talking about faith and truly live it, breathe it, and embody it. I want to thank God for everything instead of taking credit myself. I don't want to struggle through life without His guidance. Just as we, as parents, can see and know more than our children, God has the ultimate perspective. He created us; He knows exactly what He has planned for our lives. And according to our faith, it will be done.

Living By Faith

The promise of "according to your faith" isn't a one-time miracle but a daily reality. Each morning presents fresh opportunities to live from faith rather than from our fears, doubts, or limited human perspective.

This doesn't mean we'll never face struggles or that everything will always turn out exactly as we hope. But it does mean that our faith forms the container for what God can do in and through our lives. The more we expand our faith, the more space we create for divine activity.

Faith isn't about getting everything we want — it's about aligning ourselves with God's greater purposes and trusting His wisdom even when His ways confuse us. It's about knowing that even when the answer is different from what we expected, the God we trust is still good and working everything together for our ultimate good.

I've found that when I live according to my faith rather than my fears, even difficult circumstances take on new meaning. Obstacles become opportunities for God to showcase His love for us. Setbacks become setups for divine intervention.

This kind of faith-filled living doesn't happen automatically. It requires intentional practice, daily choices to trust God's promises over our circumstances, and the courage to act on what we believe rather than what we see.

How can you strengthen your faith? What obstacles might be blocking God's work through unbelief? Which parts of your life haven't been fully surrendered to Him? What would it feel like to truly live by your faith in every aspect of your life?

Your Faith-Activation Practices

Faith isn't just something we possess—it's a dynamic force we activate through intentional practice. These exercises encourage you to examine your current faith, embody trust, and recognize where your beliefs might be limiting God's work in your life. Through reflection and embodied awareness, you can turn intellectual faith into a lived experience.

1. Journal Prompt

Reflect on a time when you believed that something was impossible, but you chose to have faith anyway.

What happened?

How did your faith and belief impact the outcome?

2. Embodiment Exercise

Stand or sit with your palms facing up and imagine that in your hands, you're holding something that you desire for your life.

Now, imagine that God is ready to give you what you asked for according to your faith. Take a deep breath in and out, and say, "According to my faith, let it be done."

Now, imagine yourself receiving it in your hands.

Think about how it feels to receive your desire.

"According to your faith, let it be done to you" isn't just a statement about what's possible; it's an invitation to expand our expectations of what God can do in our lives.

Our faith forms the container for what God pours into our lives. The more we grow our faith, the more space we make for divine activity.

Today, what might change if you truly believe that what happens is directly connected to your beliefs?

Chapter 4

Touch of Faith

"Then he said to her, 'Daughter, your faith has healed you.
Go in peace." –Luke 8:48

I'm still amazed at how Scripture seems to appear in my life exactly when I need it. Sometimes it happens during a quiet walk or while I'm journaling through a struggle. At other times, I hear God speak to me in meditation, and it's clear that it's not just my inner voice. Occasionally, I'll have dreams I wake from and instantly know are connected to something I should look up and read again.

Just a few weeks ago, while deeply immersed in editing this book, I had one of those vivid, unsettling dreams. In it, I was bleeding uncontrollably from my womb. I found myself panicking in a public restroom, desperately trying to figure out how to leave without anyone noticing what was happening. The anxiety was overwhelming, and when I finally woke up, my heart was pounding so fast that I couldn't go back to sleep.

I checked my phone in the bathroom, and it was a little after 3 am. Still shaken, I knew I needed to journal and breathe deeply before my husband woke up. As I settled into this early morning reflection, suddenly, the biblical story of the bleeding woman came rushing into my mind with perfect clarity. At that moment, I knew I had to include her story in this book.

Faith in the Middle of the Night

Journal Entry, April 23, 2025

I woke up at 3 am today. I decided to stay awake and start typing. I had a strange dream last night. I was somewhere and realized I was bleeding from my womb. I wasn't in pain, but I knew something was wrong. It made me think of the story in the Bible about the woman who had been bleeding for twelve years. She had seen many doctors, spent a lot of money trying to get healed, and nothing helped.

Luke 8:43–48: And a woman was there who had been subject to bleeding for twelve years. She came up behind Him and touched the edge of His cloak, and immediately her bleeding stopped. "Who touched me?" Jesus asked. When they all denied it, Peter said, "Master, the people are crowding and pressing against you." But Jesus said, "Someone touched me; I know that power has gone out from me." Then the woman, seeing that she could not go unnoticed, came trembling and fell at His feet. In the presence of all the people, she told Him why she had touched Him and how she had been instantly healed. Then He said to her, "Daughter, your faith has healed you. Go in peace."

The interesting part of this story, and many others in the New Testament, is that her faith instantly healed her because she believed. Jesus didn't say, "I healed you." He didn't even have to do anything. He felt the healing happen without His conscious initiation. Because of the woman's faith in His ability to heal her, she was healed.

During biblical times, bleeding, especially in women, was considered unclean. We're told that she bled continuously for twelve years. She wouldn't have been able to attend the temple, and others who touched her would have been considered contaminated, according to Jewish law. We don't know if she was married or lived with family, but we can infer that, because of her condition, she was probably isolated, lonely, and unable to worship publicly. Her act of crawling on the ground to reach Jesus amid the crowd, just to touch the hem of His robe, not only showed her desperation to be healed but also her faith.

Instead of feeling upset because, by law, He now would have been contaminated by her, Jesus lovingly called her "daughter." That expression of love must have meant the world to her. He told her she was healed, to go in peace, and to live a life of peace, safety, and well-being. What a beautiful farewell. Can you imagine how her entire life changed because of her encounter with Jesus?

And this is another example of why I believe Jesus had such a profound impact on the world. The rabbinical law at the time was legalistic and kept many people separated from God by rules and restrictions. Jesus showed us that there is no separation and that we can be in communion with the living God. He was the hands and feet of God on Earth. He told us that by our faith, it will be done unto us. Not by the law, not by sacrifices, not by following the rules of the time, not by gender, caste, class, physical abilities, strength, or wealth, but by our faith.

It's interesting that this story appears in the Gospels, yet the woman remains unnamed. We don't know who she was, but her story is so important that I'm writing about it today, over 2000 years later. Her story lives on so that we can learn from it.

Why did I have this dream? I think it's because I feel like I've been searching for healing, spirituality, and a way to create and manifest outside of God for a few years. I had lost my way a bit. Maybe I had become lukewarm in my faith and lost some of my passion; now, I am on fire for God and in love with Jesus.

When Desperation Meets Faith

There's something transformative that occurs where desperation meets faith. This woman had exhausted every option. Maybe she had spent her last penny on doctors and treatments. Nothing had helped. She stood at the absolute end of her resources, her possibilities, herself.

And it was precisely at this moment of complete surrender that her faith changed everything.

I've noticed this pattern repeatedly in my journey. When I've exhausted all my efforts, wisdom, and resources, and reached my limit—that's often when faith appears most strongly. It's as if desperation removes all other choices, leaving faith as the only option.

This woman's act of reaching for Jesus's garment wasn't just a random gesture. It was a powerful display of faith born from her deepest desperation. She believed that simply touching the hem of His clothing would be enough. She didn't need a formal healing ceremony or even His direct attention. Just one touch, she believed, would change everything.

And it did.

The Courage of Faith

Think about what this woman risked. According to the laws of her time, she was unclean. Anyone she touched would become unclean. By pushing through that crowd, by reaching out to touch Jesus, she was breaking social norms and religious laws. She was risking rejection, public shaming, and possibly even punishment.

But her faith was stronger than her fear.

Sometimes, our faith calls us to act courageously, even if it seems foolish to others. It might mean quitting a secure job to follow a calling, forgiving someone who doesn't seem deserving of forgiveness, or trusting in healing even when the prognosis looks bleak.

The bleeding woman reminds us that faith often demands courage—the bravery to reach out, to do what's unconventional, and to believe when others would give up.

Desperate Faith, Divine Response

The story of the bleeding woman reminds us that sometimes, our deepest desperation becomes the catalyst for our most powerful faith. When we've exhausted all other options and tried everything in our own power, and when we've reached the end of ourselves, that's often when we reach out with the kind of faith that moves heaven.

This is the divine healing pattern—restoring our whole being, not just our visible symptoms. Jesus didn't just address her physical bleeding; He healed her isolation, restored her dignity, and gave her peace. True healing involves the body, mind, spirit, and community all at once.

Her story lives on not because she was someone special or extraordinary but because she represents all of us in our desperation, our longing, our hope against hope that reaching out to Jesus could change everything. And it did.

I love that Jesus called her "daughter." In that single word, He reversed years of loneliness, shame, and rejection. He wasn't just healing her body; He was restoring her sense of belonging, her identity, and her role in the family of God.

That's how divine healing works—it's holistic. It treats not only our immediate symptoms but the entire person. It addresses not just physical pain but also emotional wounds, social disconnection, and spiritual alienation that often accompany suffering.

As you close this chapter, remember that your moments of greatest desperation can become your purest expressions of faith. Don't hide your wounds or pretend to have everything together. Instead, bring your desperate conditions directly to Jesus, and reach out and touch the hem of His garment. According to your faith, it will be done for you.

Your Healing Touch Practices

As we reflect on this story of faith-filled desperation, I invite you to bring your own journey into this sacred space. The following practices are designed to help you shift from intellectual understanding to embodied faith. Allow yourself to approach these exercises with both vulnerability and expectation, knowing that transformation often begins with a single, courageous step.

1. Journal Prompt

The bleeding woman had tried every conventional medicine option for twelve years before reaching out to Jesus's garment. Where in your life have you been trying to solve problems through logic, control, or external solutions?

- What condition has continued despite your best efforts to fix it?
- What fears or hesitations keep you from reaching out in desperate faith?
- What one small step of faith-filled action could you take?

2. Embodiment Exercise: The Hem of the Garment Practice

Find a quiet space and set aside ten minutes of uninterrupted time.

Hold a piece of fabric (a scarf, shawl, or even the hem of your clothing) in your hands.

Close your eyes and breathe deeply. Imagine yourself as the bleeding woman, desperate for healing, willing to risk everything for just one touch of divine power.

As you hold the fabric, name aloud the specific area of your life where you need healing: "I need healing from _____."

Slowly bring the fabric to your heart, and whisper: "By faith, I receive healing. My desperation meets divine power."

Sit in stillness for two to three minutes, breathing deeply and allowing yourself to receive.

End by placing your hand on your heart and saying: "I go forth in peace, carrying this healing with me."

Journal immediately afterward about any sensations, emotions, or insights that arose during this practice.

Sometimes, our deepest desperation becomes the trigger for our most genuine faith. When we've tried everything and reached the end of ourselves, that's when we extend a kind of faith that moves heaven.

What healing might be just one touch of faith away in your life today?

Section 2

DIVINE SURRENDER

Chapter 5
New Wine, New Vessels

"And no one pours new wine into old wineskins. Otherwise, the wine will burst the skins, and both the wine and the wineskins will be ruined. No, they pour new wine into new wineskins." –Mark 2:22

There is a song called "New Wine" that I remember hearing for the first time last year. Ever since I first listened to this song, it has become my morning anthem as I brush my teeth and wash my face when I wake up. It's my intention and daily prayer to be made new. It's a reminder that as I step into my new identity and purpose, the old energy, beliefs, habits, and limitations can't come with me.

Our physical bodies are part of our spiritual selves. We are spiritual beings having a spiritual experience through this body. When I am at my best, I serve as a vessel for God. We are God's hands and feet on this Earth, in this moment, to live fully through our senses, to love, feel deeply, experience joy and pain, to grieve, to laugh, and to grow with each experience. This is one of many verses that remind us that God dwells within us and that He experiences His creation through us. How incredible is that?

Understanding New Wine

In this verse, Jesus was addressing the Pharisees, the religious leaders who struggled to accept His new teachings. The Pharisees represented the religious establishment. They were educated, studied rabbinical law, and were highly respected. Jesus, on the other hand, was just a carpenter, and what Jesus was teaching didn't align with their traditional education. The new wine here symbolizes Jesus's teachings, a new covenant, and a new way of living, while the old wineskins represent the old traditions and doctrines that were rigid and legalistic. The new wineskins are our open hearts and minds, which are needed to receive and embody Jesus's new spiritual teachings. This highlights the evolution of the New Testament teachings compared to the Old Testament.

The irony is that many of us grew up experiencing religion this way ourselves. If we grew up in the church, it might have felt legalistic, traditional, or overly dogmatic, and not relevant to our daily lives. This could be one reason why, over the past fifty years, until very recently, there has been a decline in religious affiliation and attendance at churches, synagogues, and mosques, especially among younger generations. What once worked in traditional forms of worship and structures no longer seems effective. But what can replace it? For me, it's daily alignment and connection with my Creator.

Becoming a New Vessel

I am not the winemaker or the wine; I am the wineskin. We are the vessel. The song "New Wine" talks about surrendering, letting go, and aligning with God's purpose for us in this world. Resistance has never helped me; it has always caused more pain. Being rigid, inflexible, or holding onto old thoughts, stories, or habits doesn't help me. Having attachments doesn't serve me.

This song reminds me to allow myself to be emptied so I can be refilled with more of what I need to fulfill my purpose. That involves identifying what I need to let go of. For me, it's releasing physical habits like overeating, drinking alcohol, not drinking enough water, and sleeping too little.

It's also recognizing less obvious habits or beliefs, such as people-pleasing, overachieving, perfectionism, numbing myself with Netflix after working too hard, distracting myself with busyness, and not setting healthy boundaries. It's letting go of my ego's desires, which are temporary and not focused on long-term joy, fulfillment, or impact.

I am reminded that I need to let go of what no longer serves me—or perhaps never did—so I can receive the new wine in a new wineskin. Like snakes, we must shed old versions of ourselves as we grow.

Creating Space for the New

Journal Entry, November 22, 2018

Sometimes, I feel restless. When that happens, I clean, purge, and create physical space in my surroundings. I feel overwhelmed and disappointed with myself. My house is tidy, clean, and free of clutter. I've gone through drawers, my closet, and part of the main office, hoping to donate items we no longer need. I don't understand how I haven't noticed all the "stuff" in my house. In each drawer, in every room, and in each closet, they are filled with items we've accumulated over many years that no longer serve us. My urge to purge is overwhelming. Some of these were gifts and items I've held onto for too long. It's time to simplify and, of course, correct.

My husband and I agree. We want to simplify and declutter by owning fewer things that don't bring us joy or take up unnecessary space. Since I'll be home working on this new chapter of my life, I need to create room for positive energy to flow throughout my home.

It was cathartic to go through my corporate work outfits, which are now in storage. My work clothes will go to my friend, who, after many years of consulting, is planning to return to full-time work. It makes me so happy to share my corporate wardrobe with her. I pray it will serve her well, as it has served me for over two decades.

During this process, I discovered books, beautiful cards, money, old journals, race medals, souvenirs from my trip to Hong Kong, gifts from my children when they were young, and many more treasures I had forgotten about. These meaningful items will be proudly displayed, read, and used. I will donate the items that no longer serve a purpose so the next owner can enjoy them fully.

As I go through each drawer, closet, and room, I will give thanks for every book, every paper I kept, every article of clothing, and every reminder of a moment when these items served a purpose for me. Then, I will bless them and pray that they will serve the next person who receives them.

Mark 2:22 says, "And no one pours new wine into old wineskins. Otherwise, the wine will burst the skins, and both the wine and the wineskins will be ruined. No, they pour new wine into new wineskins." It's time to make room for new wine by creating new wineskins. This means I need to examine and clean my thoughts, eating habits, and self-care practices. Just like physical things, we develop habits that need to be examined and intentionally released over time.

I look forward to sharing positive energy to make space for what God has planned for me next.

Reading that journal entry reminded me that when I'm overwhelmed, I clean and purge. I release back into the world what I no longer want or need, bless it for someone else, and, by creating more space and emptying my drawers, closets, and myself, I make room for new blessings.

The Physical Reflects the Spiritual

I was overwhelmed when I wrote that journal entry. I had given my notice that I'd be leaving my corporate job. The reality was starting to sink in that in just a few weeks, I wouldn't be going into the office at the company where I had worked for twenty-two years anymore. Instead, my office would be at home as I began my coaching and wellness business.

It was simpler to tidy up my physical space before addressing the tough stuff—my habits, mindset, and fears.

What I've realized is that our physical spaces often reflect our inner state. When my home is messy, my mind tends to be cluttered as well. When I hold onto physical objects I no longer need, I'm probably also holding onto emotional baggage that weighs me down.

The process of decluttering isn't just about creating a nicer living space—it's a spiritual practice. Every item we release creates space for something new to enter. Every old habit we break makes room for healthier patterns to emerge.

Detoxing from these habits and releasing what doesn't serve me creates space. It establishes my new wineskin, transforming me so that God can pour new wine into me. I know that if I'm not at my best, I cannot receive new blessings and won't see or appreciate them. Overindulging and overextending are sure ways to miss out on God's best.

When I realize I have fallen back into unhealthy habits, I know I've hit a plateau, am stuck, or am resisting moving to the next level. It's like I am filling myself with what I don't need to avoid what God has planned for me.

Your New Wineskin Practices

As we embrace becoming new vessels for God's purpose, I've created three practices to help you apply this principle in your daily life. These exercises will guide you in recognizing what needs to be released, visualizing your renewed self, and taking meaningful steps toward becoming a new wineskin ready to receive God's blessings.

1. Journal Prompt

What does your physical space look like? Is it cluttered? Have you accumulated more "stuff" that you don't need? Are your closets, drawers, garage, shed, and other storage areas overwhelming you?

How are your habits? Are you healthy—mentally, physically, emotionally, and spiritually? How do these habits show the growth you're truly avoiding?

Be as honest as possible. If you're not feeling great, your thoughts are especially loud, and your physical body and surroundings need some care, it's probably time to declutter, detox, and spend more time in devotion and discipline.

2. Embodiment Exercise: Becoming a New Wineskin

Sit comfortably and close your eyes.

Imagine holding a wineskin in your hands. How does it feel?

Now, picture yourself emptying it completely and releasing what no longer serves you.

See yourself filling it back up with new thoughts, new dreams, new beliefs, new possibilities. What does that feel like?

The metaphor of new wine and new wineskins reminds us that transformation isn't just additive—it's also subtractive. Sometimes the most important spiritual growth occurs not when we gain something new, but when we let go of something old.

God is always creating new things. New wine is constantly being made. The question is whether we're willing to become new vessels—flexible, expansive, and ready to receive what God wants to pour into our lives.

Will you join me in becoming a new wineskin today?

Chapter 6

God's Ways Are Higher

"For my thoughts are not your thoughts, neither are your ways my ways,"
declares the Lord. "For as the heavens are higher than the earth, so are my ways
higher than your ways and my thoughts than your thoughts." –Isaiah 55:8–9

This lesson has been a lifelong journey for me. When I face challenges in life, verses often come to mind at the right time. Sometimes, I look for verses to read, meditate on, and memorize so I can recall them exactly when I need them most. This is one of those verses.

I used to rely so heavily on myself that I would try to control outcomes and push to make things happen that I should have let go of. I'd waste time anticipating how things would turn out or planning what I needed to do to control the result. It was exhausting.

And it didn't work. It's not that I couldn't see the pattern in my behavior, but I think the conditioning was so deeply embedded in who I am that it requires more effort to loosen my grip, release control, surrender, and ask God for help. I've been rewarded and praised at home, school, and work when I figured things out on my own. That's probably why I extended that mindset to all areas of my life, without considering that God is different and that asking for help is not a sign of weakness or an inability to do things independently.

The Illusion of Control

I notice this pattern with my clients, too. We try to consider different scenarios, think through all possible options, and anticipate what might happen next, as well as why things might not work out. This is how we get stuck, delay progress, and feed our fears. Because we don't see a clear way forward or it feels too hard, we forget that God's ways are higher than ours. God's strength, power, and resourcefulness are unlike anything we have.

He reminds us in 2 Corinthians 12:9, "And he said unto me, My grace is sufficient for you: for my strength is made perfect in weakness. Therefore, I will boast all the more gladly about my weaknesses, so that Christ's power may rest on me."

In the book of Isaiah, God speaks through the prophet Isaiah to the people of Israel. At that time, the Israelites were spiritually distant from God. He is inviting them to trust in Him rather than their own understanding. He reminds them that His ways are not their ways, and His thoughts are not their thoughts. Essentially, He is God, and they are not. This message remains as relevant to me today as it was to the Israelites when it was spoken.

Why do we try to control things we can't control? Why do we worry about issues we can't influence, change, or impact? Why do we spend energy and time on circumstances outside of our control?

Meditating on these verses has given me so much freedom. Instead of relying on my understanding or what I can see or interpret with my human senses, I trust that God has a better perspective that I am not aware of and a better plan than my own.

Learning from Jesus

When I face a particularly tough day or if something in my life feels especially difficult, I think about Jesus. Being fully human while also knowing what was to come and still trusting God's will couldn't have been easy.

Jesus knew He was going to die. He prayed, "Father, if you are willing, please take this cup of suffering away from me" (Luke 22:42). Of course, as a man in human form, Jesus didn't want to be tortured and killed.

But He also prayed, "Not my will, but yours be done" (Luke 22:42). He submitted to God's will and trusted that whatever came next would serve the greatest good for everyone and fulfill a higher purpose.

Another example of how Jesus's ways differ from ours is when He was hanging on the cross. As He was actively dying, He saw the Roman soldiers gambling for His clothes, criminals hanging on the other crosses, and the crowds mocking Him and hurling insults. As a human, I imagine the physical pain, the emotional distress, and the desire to rebuke them and respond by yelling back or cursing.

Instead, Jesus did the opposite. He said, "Father, forgive them, for they do not know what they are doing" (Luke 23:34).

Reading these words always makes me cry. God's ways are not my ways. I am reminded how distant I am from the heart of God. How do I respond when someone hurts me or my family? Is my heart forgiving? Not always. While I believe we should try to imitate Jesus as a reflection of God in the flesh, this verse reminds me that I may never fully succeed in doing so.

Finding Peace in Surrender

Journal Entry, January 31, 2024

Good morning, my Lord. I feel so good today. You are working behind the scenes in my life, and you have already orchestrated everything to happen according to your design and plans. I understand that your plans are not always my plans. I love that you share Bible verses with me. I've just added another one to my book.

What a great reminder that you know better, that your ways are greater, and that you are in control.

I've learned that releasing resistance to what is makes life much simpler. Trusting that I am in control and not panicking over my circumstances brings me peace. Believing that for every obstacle, there is a detour, and every stall has a new direction, has been a blessing to me. We cannot control or foresee every step on our journey. We cannot see or feel our way out of danger. We cannot prevent heartache, grief, and pain. Nor can we imagine the blessings, beauty, love, and abundance that only God can provide.

We will always have human filters that shape how we see circumstances. We will always experience human emotions and feelings that influence our judgment and perspectives. And still, we can strive to do our best.

The Freedom of "Not Knowing"

One of the most liberating parts of accepting that God's ways are higher than ours is the freedom it gives us from feeling like we have to know everything. In our world, full of information, we often feel pressured to understand, explain, and predict everything. But this verse allows us to say, "I don't know—and that's okay."

When we face situations that don't make sense—doors closing that we expected to open, relationships ending that we thought would last, and dreams fading that we believed were from God—we can find comfort in knowing that God sees what we cannot. His perspective is higher, His timeline is longer, and His understanding is deeper.

This doesn't mean we stop seeking understanding or growth. It means we hold our understanding loosely, recognizing its limitations. We can pursue wisdom while also acknowledging that our wisdom will always be partial and incomplete compared to God's.

From Control to Trust

The journey from control to trust isn't easy, and it doesn't happen overnight. It's built through many small surrenders, and many moments of choosing to believe that God's perspective is higher than ours.

Here are some practical ways I've found to move from control to trust:

1. **Pause Before Planning**: When facing a challenge, take a moment to pray before jumping into problem-solving mode. Ask, "God, what's Your perspective on this situation?"
2. **Look for the Lesson**: When things don't go as planned, ask what you can learn from the experience instead of fixating on what went wrong.
3. **Release Outcomes**: Do your part with excellence, then consciously release your grip on how things turn out. Say aloud, "I've done what I can; I trust God with the rest."

4. **Celebrate Surprises**: When life takes unexpected turns, find the beauty or opportunity in the surprise instead of mourning your disrupted plans.
5. **Practice Gratitude**: Regularly thank God for how He has worked in your past, especially during times when His ways were higher than yours.

The more we practice these habits, the more naturally we begin to live from a place of trust rather than control. We begin to recognize the exhaustion that comes from trying to micromanage our lives and the peace that comes from surrendering to God's higher ways.

Your Higher Ways Practices

As we learn to release control and trust in God's higher ways, I've created these exercises to help you reflect on past experiences where God's perspective was clearer than yours, embody the physical sensation of surrender, and evaluate specific areas where you might still be holding on to control so you can experience the freedom that comes from trusting God's view instead of your own limited perspective.

1. Journal Prompt

Reflect on a time in your life when you were struggling with understanding why things were happening the way they were. How did you feel?

- What are you currently trying to control?
- What fears come up when you think about letting go of control?
- What might God's higher perspective be on this situation?
- What one small step could you take toward surrender?

2. Embodiment Exercise: Releasing Control

Sit or stand with your shoulders open and relaxed.

Imagine a situation in your life that feels like a heavy burden you've been carrying and feel its weight in your body.

Now imagine releasing that burden to God and watching it rise to the heavens above.

Say to yourself, "I trust that God's ways are greater than my ways."

Now, imagine replacing the burden with a newfound sense of peace. How does that feel?

The promise of Isaiah 55:8–9 isn't meant to frustrate us with our limitations—it's meant to liberate us from the heavy burden of trying to figure everything out. When we truly understand that God's ways are higher than our ways, we discover freedom from narrow perspectives and limited understanding.

This doesn't mean we'll always like God's ways or immediately understand them. It means we trust that the One who sees from heaven's perspective knows better than we do, loves us more deeply than we can comprehend, and is working all things together for good in ways we cannot yet see.

Will you join me in the lifelong journey of releasing control and embracing God's higher ways?

Chapter 7
Be Still and Know

"Be still, and know that I am God" –Psalm 46:10

I've repeated "Be still, and know that I am God" to myself for years. When I was anxious, fearful, or confused, I quietly recited it. When the world felt chaotic, frightening, and overwhelming, I prayed this verse.

When I was a young parent, unsure if I was doing the right thing, I reflected on this verse. When I had to make decisions at work that affected my team and doubted whether I knew what I was doing, I depended on this verse. When members of my family and friends received frightening health diagnoses, I reflected on this verse. When I was burned out and no longer recognized myself, I reflected on this verse and begged God for help.

A Psalm for Troubled Times

This psalm proclaims God's power, strength, and great love for us. Reading the entire chapter is helpful because it speaks directly to our world today and likely has always done so. When we look around, we see natural disasters, violence, hatred, chaos, and division. It can feel overwhelming. But God tells us not to focus on external events. Instead, retreat inward, be still, and trust that God can and will be our refuge and strength during troubling times.

I've stopped watching the news and turned off app notifications as stories come in. I realized that the content I was consuming, even from reputable sources, was designed to trigger specific emotions in me. I don't need to be constantly reminded of the lack of integrity in our leaders, the divisiveness in our country, or the darkness in senseless acts of violence.

I've found more peace by turning inward—sitting quietly in meditation, walking in nature, journaling, or reading outside while gazing at my favorite tree. I don't feel less informed; I feel protected.

Finding God in the Quiet

Sitting quietly in meditation and prayer, I feel as if I am charging myself with the greatest source of all power, wisdom, and unconditional love... because I am. My nervous system resets when I'm quiet and still, and my mind becomes calmer. It's in those moments that I hear God. During those times, I knew deep in my soul that I had to leave my career and start my own business. In those moments, I learned how to write my first book, then this one. I was told not to fear, but to trust in my Creator.

Journal Entry, December 31, 2022

I know you're celebrating your most successful year yet, and I'm so proud of you! You've grown every single day this year, and I'm proud of your progress. I saw you releasing old stories, limiting beliefs, and aligning with God on a daily basis. Your faith is stronger than ever; your hope and determination are inspiring, and you're taking good care of yourself. You're accomplishing more in less time because you're anointed. You're fulfilling your dharma, and for that, you're fully supported by God as you help many people create transformational change in their lives.

You no longer see limitations or upper limits. By listening to that still, quiet voice, you take action, and God lights your path and provides the support you need to do exceedingly and abundantly more than you can ever think or imagine. You no longer push through or try to force your way to the next levels; you breathe into them. You allow. You ask, believe, and receive. You know that nothing is more powerful than your God. 2023 was filled with incredible experiences because you realized that you are co-creating exactly what you want with God. You are, and always have been, ready and able. You finally believed it.

The world often focuses on big, grand gestures like fireworks and elaborate shows. However, God doesn't do that because He doesn't need to. He speaks to us when we step back inward, quieting external noises and sitting in silence. It's as if God takes us back to the time and place when we were in the Garden of Eden, in perfect communion and harmony with Him. When we were naked, in the garden, surrounded by nature and animals, everything was perfect. Perhaps becoming quiet helps us remember that moment.

The Power of Stillness

In our hyper-connected, constantly moving world, stillness has become an act of rebellion. We're bombarded with messages suggesting that productivity equals worth, that being busy is a badge of honor, and that staying connected is vital for success. Yet God's instruction contradicts all of this: "Be still."

Stillness isn't just the absence of movement; it's a conscious choice to pause, step back from chaos, and create space for divine connection. It's in this quiet that we remember who we are and *whose* child we are. It's where we hear the voice of God speaking through the noise of our lives.

The Hebrew word for "be still" in this verse is "raphah," which means to let go, to release, to surrender. It's not just about physical stillness but about releasing our grip on the things we're trying to control. When God says, "Be still," He's inviting us to:

- Stop striving
- Release tension
- Let go of control
- Surrender outcomes
- Rest in His presence

This stillness doesn't come naturally in our culture of constant productivity and distraction. It must be cultivated, practiced, and protected. But when we make space for it, something profound happens—we begin to "know" God in a way that intellectual understanding alone cannot provide.

Knowing Through Experience

The second part of the verse—"and know that I am God"—isn't about intellectual understanding. The Hebrew word for "know" here is "yada," which refers to intimate, experiential knowledge. It's the same word used to describe how Adam "knew" Eve. It's about relationships, not just information.

God isn't asking us to agree with a doctrine about His divinity. He's inviting us into an experience of His presence, a direct encounter with His power, love, and sovereignty. This knowing transforms us in a way that facts and doctrines alone cannot reach.

When we cultivate stillness, we create the conditions for this kind of inner knowing to grow. We shift from knowing about God *to truly knowing God*—from mere information to real transformation.

Practical Paths to Stillness

How can we practically incorporate stillness into our lives? Here are some methods that have helped me step away from chaos and into divine quiet.

1. Sacred Morning Minutes

Before checking email, news, or social media, spend five minutes being still. Take deep breaths. Listen attentively. Let God's presence be the first thing you feel each day instead of the noise of the world.

2. Nature Immersion

There's something about the natural world that soothes our inner noise. Whether it's sitting under a tree, walking by water, or tending a garden, nature pulls us into the present moment and reminds us of a power greater than ourselves.

3. Digital Sabbaths

Set regular times—whether hours or days—when you intentionally disconnect from digital devices. The constant ping of notifications keeps our nervous systems in a state of alertness, making true stillness nearly impossible.

4. Breath Prayer

Throughout your day, take thirty seconds to breathe deeply while silently repeating "Be still and know that I am God." This can serve as an anchor to help you return to your center amid life's storms.

5. Silent Retreat

Even just spending an hour at a local park or library regularly helps reset our internal rhythms and creates space for a deeper connection with the divine.

The goal isn't to add more tasks to your spiritual to-do list, but to create moments of stillness where God's presence can be felt more deeply. Even brief moments of stillness, practiced regularly, can transform how we navigate life.

Your Stillness Practices

I've developed a few practices to help you experience the power of divine stillness in your daily life. They will guide you to recognize where you most need God's peace, physically feel what sacred quiet does in your body, and find specific ways to create more space for that still, small voice in your routines. It's in these quiet moments that transformation happens — not through more effort, but by surrendering to God's loving presence.

1. Journal Prompt

When was the last time you felt anxious or scared? Is there a situation right now that's overwhelming you? What might it be like to sit quietly and listen for God's voice?

2. Embodiment Exercise: Sacred Stillness

Find a quiet spot to be with yourself, possibly on your meditation cushion or in nature.

Find your breath, and as you breathe gently and slowly, invite God to be with you.

As you think about something that makes you anxious or worried, ask God to speak to you and bring His peace. Say to yourself, "Be still and know that I am God." What did you notice?

The invitation to "be still and know that I am God" isn't just a one-time event—it's a daily practice and a way of engaging with the world that creates space for divine encounters. It doesn't require special training, elaborate rituals, or perfect circumstances—just a willingness to pause, breathe, and listen.

In a world that celebrates noise, movement, and nonstop productivity, choosing stillness becomes an act of courage and faith. It's a declaration that we trust God enough to cease our striving, that we believe His presence is more valuable than our productivity, and that we inherently know true wisdom does not come from accumulating more information but from sacred stillness.

Will you join me in accepting the invitation to be still today?

Chapter 8

His Power in Weakness

"My grace is sufficient for you, for my power is made perfect in weakness."
–2 Corinthians 12:9

I know that when I am aligned with God and fully surrender to Him, God can be at His strongest. I found this verse when I read the entire Bible for the first time in high school. I used to think it meant that when we're weak, we're unable. However, I recently looked up the biblical definition of *"weak,"* and here is what I discovered: "Weakness is a condition of being fatigued, tired, and inadequate physically, mentally, spiritually, or emotionally to the extent that you cannot function effectively." I've experienced that state of exhaustion more times than I can count.

When we are exhausted from trying to handle life on our own strength, God's power is perfect. When we are emptied, surrendered, release resistance, and stop trying to do everything ourselves, God's power becomes complete. God waits for us to surrender our attempts to do everything alone. Then, He shows His full power in our lives. This verse encourages me to surrender, rely on God, and ask for help. I often repeat it to myself because I still push, strive, and struggle until I am so weak that surrender is the only option. And then God steps in.

Paul's Thorn

When Paul spoke these words, he was speaking about his personal struggle. He was addressing the Corinthians and shared that he had a "thorn in the flesh," which represents his own personal pain or difficulty. We don't know what it is, but instead of removing this hardship, God tells him, "My grace is sufficient for you."

It might not be the answer Paul hoped for, but it's the one he got. Sometimes, God doesn't remove our struggles but instead gives us what we need each day to endure and keep going, trusting in His strength rather than our own. God is perfect in every way, which enables Him to compensate for our weaknesses.

When Control Falls Apart

When I was pregnant with our oldest daughter, Isabella, I was in my twenties. During a routine doctor's appointment, my OB-GYN was about to share the results of the blood test I took to check for any abnormalities in my pregnancy. I didn't expect anything unusual because I was young and healthy, so the chance of abnormalities seemed low. My doctor told me that the markers for Down syndrome indicated a one in eighty-six chance, which was high for my age and circumstances. I was at the appointment alone, not expecting bad news, and I remember feeling as if I had been punched in the stomach. He tried to explain that those were relatively low odds overall and that I probably shouldn't worry, but he also mentioned that if I wanted, I could choose to have an amniocentesis to find out if our baby was healthy.

Driving home, I cried in panic and called my husband, Dorel, to ask him to come home. Dorel was calmer than I was, and he said he felt like everything was going to be okay. I knew I was going to have our baby no matter what, but I also wanted the additional test done so I could prepare. I knew I loved our baby with all my heart, but I needed to know.

We went for the test, and first, you must go through genetic counseling. Then, there's a test where they insert a long needle into your abdomen and use an ultrasound to ensure they don't hit the baby. After that, I had to rest to prevent a possible miscarriage.

We waited nearly two weeks for the results. I remember praying so hard that our baby would be okay. I couldn't sleep or eat. I reacted differently than Dorel; I was upset that he seemed fine while I was falling apart.

One night, I remember lying awake, and unable to sleep. I surrendered to God that night and told Him I would be okay with whatever He had planned for us. I went to the family room and turned on the TV. As I flipped through the channels, I saw a show about families raising children with Down syndrome. I felt like God was telling me then that, regardless of the results, we would be okay, because these families were thriving, their children were happy, and they experienced joy and love. I felt lighter in that moment, as if I had let go of all resistance to what might be and turned it over to God. I let go.

The next day at work, I received a call from my doctor, who told me the test results were negative for Down syndrome or any other conditions, and that our baby was healthy. He asked if I wanted to know the baby's gender, and at that moment, I did. He said, "Your baby girl is healthy." I burst into tears of relief.

I didn't understand why we went through that experience at the time, but I knew I found rest in surrendering to God's will. I found a certainty that God would care for our family. I found peace when I stopped trying to control what was beyond my control. I found grace when I remembered that my loving Creator was holding me.

I often think back to that time when I tried to control something that wasn't mine to hold onto. I remember that God says His strength is perfected in those moments when we can no longer hold on. I realize the suffering I went through was because of my tight grip, and when I finally let go and surrendered to God, I felt the relief I had been seeking.

When Weakness Becomes Strength

There's something beautiful about how God works through our weaknesses. Our culture tells us we need to be strong, have everything together, and never show vulnerability. But God reminds us that it's when we're at our weakest—when we've exhausted all our resources, are completely worn out, and have no more solutions—that God's power flows most freely.

Why would God work this way? I think it's because:

- When I think I can handle everything on my own, I leave little space for God to work. My self-reliance blocks His help.
- When I have nowhere else to turn, I fully depend on God. My most vulnerable moments often become my most personal times with Him.

- When everyone observes the difference between what I can do and what actually happens, God's power becomes clear—not just to me, but to those around me.
- When I stop pushing and striving so hard, I create a clear path for God's power to flow freely through me.

God isn't asking me to try harder when I'm weak. He's inviting me to surrender more completely. Not to be stronger but to rely more fully on His strength. Not to figure everything out but to trust Him, who already knows exactly what lies ahead.

Living from God's Strength

What is it really like in daily life to let God's power shine through our weakness? Here are some helpful approaches I've found.

1. Be Honest About Your Limits

First, we need to be honest about where we're struggling. Where am I having a hard time? What feels too big for me? Where do I keep trying and failing?

This honest assessment isn't the end; instead, it's the start of experiencing God's power. It opens the way for Him to step in.

2. Say It Out Loud

There is something powerful about expressing our needs, whether through prayer, talking with a trusted friend, or just being honest with ourselves. "God, I can't do this alone. I need Your strength. I'm completely relying on You."

These aren't magic words that automatically fix everything, but they align our hearts with the truth and make us receptive to God's help.

3. Take Action from Trust, Not Anxiety

Even when we feel weak, we must keep moving forward. The main difference is what motivates that action. Am I moving forward out of anxiety and self-reliance, or because of trust in God?

The actions might seem similar on the surface, but they feel entirely different inside. One drains us; the other energizes us. One causes stress; the other brings peace, even during tough times.

4. Change How You Define Success

When we rely on God's power instead of our own, success looks different. Success becomes faithfulness rather than achievement, obedience rather than results, and trust rather than control.

This change frees us from the overwhelming pressure to be perfect and lets us rest in the knowledge that God is in control of the outcomes.

5. Be Grateful for Your Weaknesses

Instead of resenting or hiding our weaknesses, we can be thankful for how they bring us closer to God. This doesn't mean we enjoy suffering, but we recognize the opportunity these challenges give us to experience God's power.

Paul himself demonstrated this when he wrote, "Therefore I will boast all the more gladly about my weaknesses, so that Christ's power may rest on me" (2 Corinthians 12:9b).

Your Divine Strength Practices

I've created these practices to help you experience God's power flowing through your weaknesses. They will guide you to remember times when God's grace was enough, truly feel what surrendering is in your body, and recognize where you might be exhausting yourself trying to do everything on your own. God shows up most powerfully not when we have everything together, but when we finally admit we don't.

1. Journal Prompt

Reflect on a time when God's grace was enough for you. When did you feel weak, insufficient, or unprepared to handle something? How did God support you?

Are there areas you're trying to control on your own right now?

Is there an opportunity to invite God into them?

2. Embodiment Exercise: Surrender to God's Power

Make yourself comfortable, close your eyes, and take slow breaths.

Consider an area in your life where you feel inadequate or lacking.

As you breathe, imagine yourself letting go of the need to be strong and handle everything alone.

Invite God in to support you and help you face your challenges. What does it feel like to surrender to God and let His strength work through your weakness?

The promise of 2 Corinthians 12:9 isn't that God will remove our weaknesses or make all our problems disappear. It's that His grace—His unearned favor and empowering presence—is sufficient, even when our circumstances stay difficult.

His power shines most brightly through the cracks of our imperfections. Our limitations become the very places where divine strength is most clearly demonstrated. Our inadequacies become the canvas on which God portrays His sufficiency.

Today, no matter what weakness you face, what inadequacy you feel, or what challenge seems beyond your ability—it's in that very place that God's power is ready to be made perfect.

Will you open your hands, loosen your tight grip on control, and allow divine strength to flow through you?

Chapter 9

The Yoke of Rest

"Come to me, all you who are weary and burdened, and I will give you rest. Take my yoke upon you and learn from me, for I am gentle and humble in heart, and you will find rest for your souls. For my yoke is easy, and my burden is light." –Matthew 11:28–30

This should be a daily reminder for me. When I read this verse, I can feel my breath slow down, my shoulders relax, and the space in my heart begin to expand. My natural tendency is to run hard from the moment I open my eyes until I close them again at night. I don't know if this is a result of conditioning or how I'm wired, but this tendency gets me into trouble as often as it is praised.

My husband jokes that I overcommit, overextend, and squeeze every ounce of productivity out of each day. As a result, I often push myself to the point of exhaustion. When I'm tired and in need of rest, I also need a reminder to turn to God. The idea of finding rest for my soul sounds so peaceful, so why do I forget that I don't have to face everything alone?

Understanding the Yoke

When Jesus shared this message, the people He was ministering to were tired and burdened. The religious laws were strict and hard to follow, and the Romans taxed the citizens heavily. When Jesus used the word "yoke," it created a strong image. A yoke is a wooden frame placed on animals' shoulders to help them pull heavy loads. This probably reflected how the people Jesus was speaking to felt, as if they were carrying heavy burdens and dragging heavy loads behind them.

Jesus acknowledged their pain and feelings and, in contrast, told them that His yoke is easy and the burden is light. Can you imagine the relief and maybe even disbelief they must have felt when hearing these words?

It's overwhelming to think that, while Jesus spoke these words to His disciples and followers, He knew He would be carrying His cross to His crucifixion. He'd bear the 300 lb. cross for a third of a mile, or roughly 600 meters. He would literally feel the weight of our burdens. This image, compared to my burdens, brings me to my knees.

Learning to Rest

When I meditate on these words, I am reminded that we're not meant to navigate life alone. We were created to be in communion with God, our Creator. He breathed life into us. Although we distract ourselves and suppress the Holy Spirit, He remains within us. His yoke is light and easy.

When I wake up early in the morning before the sun rises, I spend most of my time at the feet of God. I rest in His presence. He waits for me. I sit on my cushion in the dark, cross-legged, and cover my head with a blanket or prayer shawl. I find it comforting to pray, worship, and meditate this way. I feel like my energy is contained; the darkness in my office at 5 am helps me turn inward, creating more focus and stillness. There, I can hear the calm, quiet voice of God. There, I exhale. There, I breathe more easily. There, I feel God's presence within me and all around me. There, I am in communion.

My Journey from Striving to Rest

I've endured weariness and a heavy sense of burden throughout my life. I've neglected to give myself the rest I desperately needed when it was most crucial. My parents and grandparents demonstrated relentless hard work, even when it pushed them beyond exhaustion. I inherited these traits and took pride in working hard. I first practiced this while trying to catch up to other kids in school who grew up speaking English as their primary language. They had an advantage, and I worked hard not only to catch up but also to surpass and excel academically. It helped that I had an insatiable curiosity and loved learning. Once I learned to read, I never stopped.

I wasn't the smartest kid in school, but I was curious, loved learning, and worked very hard. I enjoyed earning approval from my parents, grandparents, and teachers. I was addicted to that validation, and my self-esteem depended on my GPA, awards, and any other measurable achievements.

As an adult, I maintained this pace throughout my career. I was married, raising two children, and attending graduate school full-time, often sacrificing sleep to manage everything without disappointing anyone. One of my closest friends, Marinika, who recently passed away, always told me to relax, slow down, enjoy life, and take time to rest.

During my corporate days, I worked seven days a week to keep up with job demands while feeling guilty for not being fully present with my kids and husband. I reached a breaking point one day when I couldn't keep up with working every single day. I broke down and cried out to God, "I can't do this anymore. I will begin keeping the Sabbath, but I need you to help me finish everything in the other days." And He did.

I realized that God was waiting for me to ask for His help. He promised we could come to Him, but I never did. I forgot that I'm not alone and don't have to carry burdens by myself. I forgot that while my abilities are limited, God is limitless.

The Invitation to Exchange Yokes

When I found this verse, I recited it to myself whenever I felt overwhelmed, tired, or realized that I was trying to do everything alone. I don't think God needs to be reminded that He promised this, but I say it with conviction and then let go and surrender.

My dear friend, Marinika, passed away two years ago. Although her life was short in years, it was deeply meaningful. She embraced everything life offered—her sons, family, friends, the lake, her morning walks, and even the strangers she'd meet along the way. Her faith wasn't something separate from her life; she lived God's promises every single day.

I keep her picture on my desk where I see it first thing every morning. She continues to teach me and remind me to slow down, rest, sit quietly, and spend more time in nature. She saw right through my pattern of pushing too hard until I crashed, resting just enough, then jumping back into the cycle.

Marinika lived in beautiful surrender to what is, finding joy in everyday moments as she "hugged the lake" during her park walks. I'm still working to follow her example. She understood that Jesus's yoke was easy—a lesson I'm learning day by day.

The Legacy of a Life

Journal Entry, July 5, 2023

Yesterday was a tough day. My heart felt so heavy thinking of my Fina Marinika. What is the legacy of a life? When someone passes away, we see what their legacy was. Everyone who has talked about Marinika remembers her as vibrant, fun, and joyful. We recall her smile and laughter. I remember her cooking for her kids. I remember the signs all around her house bearing messages of love, kindness, and respect. I recall sitting on her porch, talking, drinking coffee or tea. I remember working at KeyBank and going out for Happy Hour. I remember how much she loved her boys.

I remember her faith, her conversations with God, her care for others, her willingness to take in strangers, and her ability to make them feel like friends. I remember how she always remembered birthdays and anniversaries. I remember how grateful she was for everything she had. She took better care of everything than anyone I know.

I remember how she always told me to slow down. When she was younger, she was quick, too. She walked fast, achieved a lot, but after she got sick, she slowed down. She savored every moment. She was fully present. She connected with God and nature every day. She loved everyone deeply. She told me to breathe, to do less, to rest more. She was an example for me of someone who relied on God in every moment.

The Counterintuitive Nature of Rest

One of the most beautiful paradoxes in Jesus's teaching is that taking His yoke, which seems like adding weight, actually eases our burden. This contradicts our natural thinking. How can adding a yoke bring rest?

The difference is that Jesus's yoke is not like the other yokes we typically wear. Most of us carry yokes of:

- Performance (trying to prove our worth)
- Perfectionism (never allowing mistakes)
- People-pleasing (fearing disapproval)
- Self-reliance (believing it all depends on us)

These yokes exhaust us because they were never made for human shoulders. They demand more than we can sustainably give.

In contrast, Jesus's yoke is made for each of us. It distributes the weight evenly. It doesn't add any burden. Most importantly, it's a shared yoke—Jesus stands on the other side of the frame, bearing the heavier load.

This invitation to exchange yokes isn't about adding spiritual obligations to our already busy lives. It's about swapping our heavy solo burdens for a balanced, shared connection with the divine.

Practical Ways to Accept Jesus's Yoke

What does accepting Jesus's invitation to rest look like in daily life? Here are some ways that have helped me transition from exhaustion to rest.

1. Identify Your Current Yoke

What is really causing your exhaustion? Is it the work itself or the meaning you've attached to it? Is it the pace or the pressure to perform perfectly? Is it the responsibilities or the fear of letting others down?

Getting clear on what's really weighing you down helps you understand what to let go of.

2. Practice Regular Release

Create rituals of release—daily, weekly, and seasonal. For me, morning meditation, prayer, and walks outside serve as daily releases. The Sabbath provides a weekly release. Retreats act as seasonal releases.

These aren't simply pauses in activity but intentional releases of burden.

3. Reimagine Productivity

Rest isn't just the absence of work but a different kind of productivity. It produces things that work cannot: perspective, wisdom, creativity, connection, healing.

I've found that my most productive insights often come during or after periods of true rest.

4. Allow for Divine Partnership

Jesus not only offers to take our burdens away, but He also works alongside us, showing us how to carry what we must with grace and ease.

This means tackling tasks with an awareness of divine partnership instead of solo effort.

5. Create Margins

A life without margins is a life that can't afford rest. Start creating margins by saying no, simplifying, and intentionally leaving some space empty. Consider them sacred boundaries.

I've realized that what I *don't* plan is often just as important as what I do.

Your Rest Practices

I've created these practices to help you experience the lighter yoke Jesus offers. These will guide you to identify your heaviest burdens, physically feel the exchange of yokes in your body, and assess specific areas where you might be carrying weight alone that was meant to be shared. Remember, proper rest isn't found in doing nothing—it's found in doing life together with God.

1. Journal Prompt

Which parts of your life make you feel tired or weighed down?

What burden feels the heaviest?

How can you take on Jesus's easy yoke and receive His rest?

2. Embodiment Exercise: Exchanging Yokes

Find a peaceful spot, sit comfortably, and close your eyes.

Find your breath and start to breathe deeply and slowly. As you breathe, invite any heaviness to leave your body with each exhale. As you breathe out, picture any heaviness, tiredness, or burdens being released and given over to God.

Now imagine Jesus's yoke around you. Feel its lightness and a sense of relief flow through your body.

As you breathe, welcome peace, calm, and grace. What did you notice when you surrendered?

The invitation in Matthew 11:28–30 isn't just about temporary relief from life's pressures. It's about a fundamentally different way of living, where we don't carry life's burdens alone but partner with God.

This doesn't mean our responsibilities disappear or that life suddenly becomes easy. It means we approach those responsibilities differently— sharing divine partnership instead of trying alone, from a mindset of spiritual abundance rather than personal lack.

Today, what heavy yoke can you exchange for the lighter one Jesus offers? What burden have you been carrying alone that was meant to be shared? What exhaustion might be transformed into rest if you accept this ancient invitation?

The offer stands, "Come to me...and I will give you rest."

Chapter 10

Renewed in Mind

"Therefore, I urge you, brothers and sisters, in view of God's mercy, to offer your bodies as a living sacrifice, holy and pleasing to God—this is your true and proper worship. Do not conform to the pattern of this world, but be transformed by the renewing of your mind."
–Romans 12:1–2

I spend a lot of time dwelling on my thoughts. And yes, many of my thoughts are the same fears, unkind words, and chaotic distractions that keep me stuck. My struggle isn't unique. Many of us feel disconnected from our bodies. We live in our minds, and often, the thoughts we allow to loop are unkind, judgmental, critical, and rooted in past conditioning. Studies show that we have between 50,000 to 80,000 thoughts each day. Most are negative and repetitive.

We also face intense pressure to conform to the dominant worldview. This verse reminds us that we don't need to follow the pattern of this world, but to be transformed by renewing our minds. How powerful is that? In the spiritual realm, we often hear that thoughts become things. Here is Scripture that essentially shares the same message.

Paul's Call to Transformation

When Paul wrote these words, he was addressing the Roman Christians. He encouraged them to stay committed to their faith, even when facing pressure and struggles to conform to the world, which might conflict with their beliefs. He urges them, and us, to live our lives as the embodiment of our faith and to be renewed daily in our minds. It's not a one-time action we can take, but rather the daily choices we make.

And the struggle is real for all of us. Our inner dialogue and programming run constantly, even while we sleep. Have you ever woken up in the middle of the night and realized you're still thinking about what you went to bed with? Or wake up in the morning with the same thoughts?

This verse encourages us to be transformed by renewing our minds. For me, this means deliberately choosing to focus not on negative thoughts, worries, or fears, but instead on the fact that we are vessels through which God can do great things in this world. To do that, I need to take better care of myself—mentally, physically, emotionally, and spiritually.

Daily Renewal Practices

I have started a morning and evening habit of writing gratitude and affirmations in a notebook. I keep my beautiful notebook and a pouch filled with various colored pens and markers on my nightstand. I look forward to doing this in bed, both in the mornings and evenings. Choosing to give thanks for the blessings in my life and affirming what I believe for my future, even if it's not yet visible in the physical world, is an extension of my faith. It's like having a conversation with God where I share what's on my heart and acknowledge that He already knows.

Journal Entry, January 1, 2024

It's a new year, a new day, and an opportunity to start fresh with intention. I am very excited for this year. My word is EMBODIED. I embody all that I am and who I know God created me to BE. I will feel it all, embody it all, see it all, savor it all, and appreciate it all. I am leaving behind worries, doubts, struggles, striving, and the pursuit of achievement. I run toward God, stay aligned, and seek to hear that still, quiet voice that resides within. I do this by drinking water, sleeping more, resting, sitting still, listening, and allowing God to create through me.

I keep my vessel clean and pure so that the Holy Spirit has more space to fill me with the divine. I don't seek to cloud, numb, or escape. I seek to be ALIVE, EMBODIED! I seek curiosity. I seek miracles. I seek blessings. I notice it all. I feel it all. I am it all. This year is different. So today, I walk outside, plan, clear clutter, and make room for new energy. I am ready!

2023 was a year full of highlights for me, but I also ended it feeling physically, emotionally, and mentally drained. My old habits crept back in—striving, pushing, working hard, trying desperately to reach all my goals. And much of it was positive. I traveled extensively in 2023, achieved many of my business milestones, and experienced spiritual growth. I connected with God more powerfully each day. Through that growth, I realized how often I still default to relying on myself. I also felt time slipping away faster than ever before. This year felt like the fastest of my life. So, I plan to do things differently in the coming year.

I sense God urging me to slow down, to feel deeply—the good and the difficult. I am called again to simplify, to eliminate clutter and distractions, to create space for God to work His magic.

That's what this verse reminds me of: God is capable of more than we can think or imagine. God can do more than I could ever accomplish on my own, so I choose to live that way. It will require me to surrender constantly, not just daily, but in each moment. I release old habits, many of which have brought me to where I am, but I know they can only take me so far. I no longer want to pull this heavy weight behind me when I know there's a better way.

So, I can devote more time to prayer, communion, and alignment with God—sitting, worshiping, listening, and praising. I can take better care of myself—because I am the soil—and God is the gardener who cultivates the seed. If my soil isn't healthy, God's blessings won't take root deeply in me, and they won't bear fruit.

This requires me to make different choices about what I consume — from the food I eat to what I drink, the amount of sleep and rest I give myself, my daily activity, and how I nourish my mind and spirit — all of it. It calls for discernment in what I contribute to the world. My spiritual energy directly reflects my daily choices.

If I don't take better care of myself as a vessel that holds the Holy Spirit and allows the divine to work through me, I won't reach the full potential that God has created me for. Like anything else, it requires some deep cleaning and daily maintenance. It requires me to check in regularly and recommit to this way of life.

I'm excited to let God guide, direct, and work through me. I look forward to seeing what flows from this partnership and collaboration. I used to make plans and share them with God, asking Him to bless or accelerate them. Now I strive to EMBODY who He made me to be, so I can ALLOW His creation and genius to shine through me. For His ways are greater than my ways, His plans are bigger than mine, and His power is made perfect in my weakness.

Instead of feeling scared or worried, I feel more relaxed than ever because I trust in His promises. I am stepping aside so God, who is LIMITLESS, can display His beauty through me to the world.

I refuse to follow the patterns of a world that is now chaotic, anxious, polarized, negative, and unhealthy. I choose to be changed by renewing my mind. My life and how I present myself in this world reflect my faith. It's how I show what I believe. It's me doing my part to make the world a kinder, more loving, and more compassionate place.

The Body-Mind Connection

What I find fascinating about Paul's words is how he connects the physical body with mental renewal. He doesn't separate them as our culture often does. He begins by urging us to "offer your bodies as a living sacrifice" and then mentions "the renewing of your mind." This suggests a profound connection between physical and mental/spiritual practices.

In my own life, I've noticed that neglecting one part of myself causes other parts to suffer as well. When I don't properly care for my body—such as neglecting my sleep, nutrition, movement, or rest—my mental health also declines. And, when my mind is filled with anxious thoughts, my body experiences stress and tension. They are interconnected parts of the same whole.

This holistic perspective prompts me to view my physical self-care not as vanity or indulgence but as a sacred responsibility. The body isn't separate from spiritual life—it's an essential part of it. When I attend to my physical needs with intention and respect, I also nurture mental renewal.

Breaking Worldly Thought Patterns

The phrase "do not conform to the pattern of this world" encourages further reflection. What are the thought patterns in our world today that might be influencing us unconsciously?

Some deeply rooted thought patterns I've had to intentionally break free from include:

1. Productivity Above Presence

Our culture often focuses more on what we produce than on who we are. Our worth becomes connected to output, efficiency, and visible accomplishments. This mindset drives the constant hustle, burnout, and guilt we experience when we rest.

Renewing my mind means accepting the truth that my worth isn't determined by what I do but by who I am and *whom* I belong to. I am fully valued by God regardless of my achievements.

2. Comparison and Competition

Social media and consumer culture constantly encourage comparison. We compare our inner selves to others' appearances, our beginnings to others' midpoints, and our struggles to others' highlight reels.

Renewing my mind means embracing the truth that my path is uniquely mine. God's plans for me aren't affected by others' success or failure.

3. Scarcity and Fear

The world constantly sends messages of "not enough"—not enough time, money, security, status, or love. This scarcity mindset fuels anxiety, hoarding, relentless effort, and mistrust.

Renewing my mind involves adopting an abundance mindset—not in a materialistic way, but by recognizing God's provision, presence, and sufficiency in every situation.

4. Instant Gratification

Our culture prioritizes instant results and quick fixes. We seek transformation without effort, wisdom without learning, and success without facing challenges or setbacks.

Renewing my mind means trusting divine timing and the growth process, even when it feels slower than I expect.

5. Self-Reliance

Maybe the most challenging part for me has been letting go of the deeply ingrained belief that everything depends on me. This pattern of self-reliance might seem like a strength, but it actually reveals a lack of trust.

Renewing my mind means relying on God—not as a sign of weakness but as the true source of strength and effectiveness.

Practical Mind Renewal

How can we actively participate in this renewal process? Here are some strategies that have helped me make room for divine transformation.

1. Input Management

Our minds are shaped by what we consistently expose them to. Choosing carefully what I read, watch, listen to, and who I spend time with has been essential for my renewal.

This isn't about living in a bubble, but it does mean being intentional with my mental diet. Just as I wouldn't expect physical health while constantly eating junk food, I can't expect mental renewal while consuming toxic content.

2. Pattern Interruption

Whenever I notice myself spiraling into negative thoughts, I've learned to interrupt the cycle. This might involve reciting Scripture aloud, moving physically, changing environments, or simply naming the pattern of thoughts I'm in.

These pauses help me intentionally connect with God instead of reacting automatically.

3. Intentional Replacement

Our minds struggle with empty spaces. When we try to stop thinking negative thoughts without replacing them with something better, our minds automatically fill the void, often with the same old patterns. It's not enough to stop negative thoughts; I need to intentionally replace them with truth. That's why Paul follows his "do not" with a "but" that points to the positive alternative.

Memorized Scripture, positive affirmations, and truth statements become my go-to focus when I notice my mind drifting into unhelpful territory.

4. Community Reinforcement

I've noticed that my mind refreshes more quickly and deeply when I am around others on the same journey. Hearing my friends or community speak the truth strengthens my own growth.

This is why I make sure to spend time with people who support and challenge me rather than pull me back into worldly patterns.

5. Physical Practices

Honoring the body-mind connection, I've included physical practices that encourage mental renewal, such as getting enough sleep, eating nourishing foods, engaging in joyful movement, spending time in nature, and taking moments of stillness.

These practices aren't separate from spiritual disciplines but complement them to foster transformation.

Your Mind Renewal Practices

These practices are meant to help you clear your mind and let go of worldly thought patterns. They guide you in understanding what it truly means to live your faith, experience divine harmony in your body, and recognize the specific thought patterns that hold you back. Renewal isn't something you do just once and check off your list; it's a daily choice to partner with God in reshaping your thoughts, one moment at a time.

1. Journal Prompt

What does it mean to live your life as a reflection of your faith? How do you show your faith every day through your thoughts, words, deeds, and actions?

How can you change your thoughts every day?

2. Embodiment Exercise: Mind Renewal

Sit quietly, close your eyes, and focus on your breath.

Reflect on an area of your life you'd like to change—whether it's a relationship, a work situation, a personal habit, or negative thoughts—and bring it before God.

Now, visualize God taking it and renewing your thinking to align with what is more in line with Him.

What does it feel like to be in alignment with God?

Romans 12:1–2 isn't just telling us to think more positively. It's calling us into a complete transformation that starts in our minds and touches every part of our lives.

We can't achieve this with willpower alone. It's a partnership where we make space through our practices, but God performs the actual transformation.

Today, which worldly thought patterns are you ready to break free from? What truth from God is prepared to take hold in your mind? What small practice might open the way for this transformation?

The world will always pressure us to conform. However, you can choose a different path where your mind is constantly renewed, leading to beautiful transformation.

Section 3

PURPOSE & CALLING

Chapter 11
The Narrow Path

"Enter through the narrow gate. For wide is the gate, and broad is the road that leads to destruction, and many enter through it. But small is the gate and narrow the road that leads to life, and only a few find it." –Matthew 7:13–14

This verse might be where my understanding has changed the most over the years. I used to believe the narrow path was the more difficult, stricter one, but over time, I've come to see it differently. When we first arrived in the States, I desperately wanted to fit in. My young mind thought that erasing everything that made me feel different and blending into this culture was the answer. I desperately wanted to have long, smooth, straight hair like my friend Susie's. She wore t-shirts, jeans, and sneakers and was the picture of elementary school style. I was not that.

I wanted to feel like I belonged, and I enjoyed being recognized for my achievements and dedication to excellence, whether at home, in school, or at work. I believed that external validation and praise would make me happy, but they didn't. I still felt different and struggled to find a true sense of belonging. A deep sense of belonging has been, and continues to be, one of my biggest challenges.

Seeking Belonging

This struggle between fitting in and staying true to ourselves reflects what Jesus discusses in this verse from the Sermon on the Mount. He presents a contrast between two paths, two choices we face in life. We can follow our desires and those of the world (the wide gate), or we can choose to follow God's will (the narrow gate). He encourages the crowd to pick the narrow gate, which leads to God's will, instead of the wide gate, which brings destruction through worldly expectations and conformity.

The place where I always felt I belonged was in my relationship with God. Since I was young, I loved reading Scripture with my grandmother. I would sit next to her as she read from her Bible and share my thoughts on what it meant. Showing me that I could connect with the living Word and interpret it on my own was a true gift. Now I see that I wasn't afraid to read the Bible. I didn't think it was only for priests, pastors, or rabbis. It was alive for me, too.

Finding My Way

I read the entire Bible for the first time in high school. I started with Genesis and finished with Revelation. I read straight through, and it felt good. I experienced a deep sense of belonging during those quiet moments in the Word. I realize that I am loved exactly as I am, just for being myself. Over time, I allowed my true self to show more often, but I still adjusted for settings where I didn't feel like everyone else.

I saw college as a place for exploration. I was an English literature major with minors in French and women's studies. Why? Because that's what I wanted to study. I took philosophy, anthropology, sociology, psychology, every literature class I could find, Italian, linguistics, and comparative religion, and loved every minute of it. I enjoyed taking any classes I wanted. I felt nourished. When I backpacked around Europe after graduation, I felt alive, free, and completely myself. Looking back, I see how this time was my attempt to find and follow my own narrow path, guided by what truly resonated with my spirit.

When it was time to find a job, I felt like my time was up, and I had to take my career and life seriously. I took a traditional route in my career. It was as if I was snapped back into making choices that everyone else did. I decided to act like a grown-up and do what everyone else did, too. I worked for a financial institution where I could grow in my career, work hard, get promoted, and stay there until retirement. I cut my long, curly hair into a short bob, bought Ann Taylor suits and pumps, and dressed the part. I spent twenty-five years in the corporate world.

Choosing the Wide Gate

I entered through the wide gate. Looking back, I realize I was living life at the bank as a persona, not truly myself. I was playing a role, having abandoned the narrow path of authenticity for the broad road of cultural expectations and external definitions of success. Over time, I knew I couldn't wait any longer and decided to live differently. Because of that decision, you're reading these words today. I don't believe I could have pursued what I'm doing now if I hadn't left that wide-gate life behind and rediscovered my true path.

This verse reminds me not to follow others blindly but to be discerning in my choices and to prioritize alignment over validation. It's tempting to go along with the crowd and want what others have, but we are not meant to take the wide gate and broad road. When I was younger, I thought this verse meant resisting peer pressure and avoiding harmful choices, like drinking too much, experimenting with drugs, or being in unhealthy relationships. Don't feel pressured to do what everyone else is doing just to fit in if it doesn't feel right.

I used to think the narrow gate meant going to church, reading the Bible, being good, following rules, and obeying my parents. It sounded tougher and less fun, but probably the "right" thing to do. However, I don't believe this verse only applies to those choices.

The Narrow Way

In my life, choosing the narrow gate involves paying attention to what I focus on. Am I looking outward to the world or inward for guidance and direction? What am I worshiping? Is it what society considers important, or what I know in my Spirit to be true? Am I creating a life that aligns with my values and purpose, or one defined by others as successful?

God promises to speak through that quiet, still voice inside us. The small gate and narrow road are harder to find—perhaps less grand, less showy, and not as obvious—but they are the ones leading to life. When we quiet ourselves and become still, we hear the whisper or see the light. Follow that path to discover a more meaningful and impactful life. It took me twenty-five years in the corporate world to rediscover this truth, but the joy and purpose I've found since choosing the narrow path again confirm what Jesus promised—this is indeed the way that leads to life.

I left corporate life in January 2019. A few months later, this is how I felt:

Freedom

Journal Entry, September 26, 2019

I've never experienced this feeling before. It's a weightless sensation that stays with me all day. I feel in flow with my work, my heart feels so full of love, and my eyes sometimes well up. I'm in a constant state of gratitude. I thank God throughout the day for the butterfly that visited my patio, the rustling leaves, the wind's howl, the birds outside my window, the home I cherish, and the thought of my family and friends who bring me great happiness. Other worries and thoughts have been replaced with pure joy, hope, and peace.

This must be the alignment and connection with God that I've read about. I have officially said goodbye to grief and fear, and I've chosen to focus on my passion and mission of helping others create transformational change in their lives. People are reaching out to connect; others I've contacted agree to meet. I am booking jobs, and the work feels effortless.

I feel like I'm noticing things around me that have always been there, but I've never seen them before. I am completely and fully present in the moment, not focused on yesterday or tomorrow, or months from now. Just right here, right now. This makes my conversations more engaging and meaningful. It also means that I cry more easily, probably stare too intently, and may seem a little odd.

I am co-creating this big, bold, beautiful, authentic life with God. I am not the same person I was before; I have shed layers of protection that are no longer needed and no longer serve me. What is emerging is my true Self, with a capital "S." I used to think I had lost my identity, but I hadn't. I never really knew my true essence. I had been different things, at various times in my life. My husband, my children, and those closest to me have all noticed a change in me.

84

Now that I've reached this new level, it's time to share with others and add more value in this world.

Your Path Practices

These practices will help you reflect on your current choices, visualize what true alignment feels like in your body, and assess specific areas where you might be following the crowd instead of God's unique calling for your life. Choosing the narrow path isn't about restriction—it's about the freedom that comes when you finally stop trying to be someone else and fully embrace who God created you to be.

1. Journal Prompt

Have you chosen the wide or narrow path?

What does it look like to live your life according to God's will?

2. Embodiment Practice: Visualizing Your Path

Find a quiet spot, sit comfortably, and focus on your breath. Take a few deep breaths to ground yourself and connect with your body.

Imagine two paths before you: one that is wide and full of worldly promises, and another that is narrow, representing God's will for your life to align with your values and purpose, and His will.

What is it like to go through the narrow gate? What would you need to leave behind?

The choice between these two paths isn't just a one-time decision, but a daily commitment. Each morning, we have opportunities to choose again—to follow the crowd or to listen for that still, small voice guiding us toward what truly matters.

The narrow path isn't about strict rule-following or joyless restrictions. It's about authentic alignment with who you are meant to be. It's about releasing what the world tells you to desire and embracing what your soul truly needs. It's about discovering your deepest sense of belonging, not through external validation but in connection with your Creator.

Your journey toward the narrow gate begins with a single step. Will you choose it today?

Chapter 12
God's Handiwork

"For we are God's handiwork, created in Christ Jesus to do good works, which God prepared in advance for us to do." –Ephesians 2:10

As humans, we often feel the need to be ready, prepared, earn more certifications, learn more, boost our credibility, and build our confidence, among other things. We believe we must prove our worth through achievement, external validation, and our work. Jesus does not call the qualified; instead, He qualifies the called. He has already qualified us to do the work He has placed on our hearts.

I remember reading this sentence in the book *Chase the Lion,* and something clicked. God isn't waiting for us to do more to use us. This validation gave me the courage to pursue the things He gave me a passion for, like starting my business, writing my books, launching a podcast, hosting retreats, speaking on stages, and taking action before I felt ready—because He says that He has prepared them in advance for me.

Called and Qualified

God has repeatedly shown us in Scripture that He chooses people others might overlook to do His work. Before He was ready, God selected Moses to lead His people. God spoke to Moses at the burning bush, but He had been preparing him for decades in Egypt, equipping him with the leadership skills he needed. During his time in the wilderness, he had to rely on God, and even his stutter demonstrated that God's power would be more apparent when he spoke. Every experience was preparation, even the ones that seemed like setbacks.

David was anointed as king while still a boy watching sheep, but every experience he encountered in the fields prepared him for Goliath. His heart for worship, even when alone in the fields, was shaping him to be a king after God's own heart.

Peter, the fisherman with a quick temper, was exactly who Jesus needed to lead the early church. When the Holy Spirit energized Peter's passion, it ignited the fire that sparked a movement. Despite his weaknesses, his love for Jesus and his boldness enabled him to lead despite his fears.

God chose each of us because He created us. We are the hands and feet of God. I believe He did this intentionally to show us that God can do great things through imperfect people, just like us. It's not about us or what we can do; it's about us stepping aside so God can work through us for the greatest good of all.

The Already and Not Yet

You are both God's finished masterpiece and His ongoing work in progress. You are completely loved, accepted, and qualified by Christ. And you're still growing, learning, and becoming everything He designed you to be.

You can step into your calling now. You don't have to wait until you feel ready because readiness isn't the requirement; obedience is. You don't need to be perfect, you just have to say "yes."

Paul wrote these words in his letter to the Ephesians to encourage them and remind them of their new identity in Christ. Because of their faith, they were made new. They are no longer who they used to be. He reminds them that they were created perfectly in God's image to do good works on His behalf.

We make it about us and forget that we are vessels through which God does His work. We were created to do good work. The ego makes it about us. We forget that we have the spirit of the Creator of the Universe inside of us—a torch of light, love, and energy to better this world.

Never Enough

For years, I didn't think I was good enough. It started with feeling behind in school because I didn't learn English until kindergarten and only caught up by second grade. I worked very hard, feeling like I was on the outside looking in. I was embarrassed to be in the lowest reading group, which included me and three boys with behavioral issues. By the end of first grade, when I was moved up to the middle group, I felt so proud and happy. I felt like I could finally breathe. Then, I decided I wanted to be in the highest reading group. I wasn't going to stop until I felt like I belonged there. I wasn't sure if I was smart enough, but I knew I could work really hard. By second grade, I was earning straight As with no help from anyone at home.

I believe that drive to succeed has continued ever since that day. I always wanted to prove myself. Validation and recognition were my addictions; they were signs that I belonged and that I was enough.

For years, I worked in banking and never felt like I truly belonged. I had a liberal arts degree, while my peers had business degrees. I decided to go to graduate school to earn my MBA and gain the credibility and validation I needed to prove that I belonged.

I've always struggled with feeling like I don't belong, believing that people don't like me, that I'm not enough, or that I'm falling behind. I guess that part of me never fully healed. I was worried when I started my own business that I would have to post on social media and be seen clearly. I realized that I have a problem with being seen because of a fear of what others might think. All this striving and proving was the opposite of what Paul writes about in Ephesians. Instead of resting in my identity as God's handiwork, I was trying to create my own sense of worth.

Finding Courage

Gradually, I started posting on social media. One day, I shared a picture of myself on LinkedIn, and an acquaintance from my corporate days sent me a message saying he thought it was a video and suggested I should post a video if I hadn't yet, because people wanted to hear from me. He confirmed that my thoughts mattered. So, I did, and although it was scary, it turned out to be a positive experience.

That very person died unexpectedly of a heart attack before we could plan our next coffee date. He was about my age, had a family, and was living life on his own terms. He had just written a book, was helping young kids get into college, and was speaking at events. His passing reminded me that nothing is guaranteed in this life, and that we can't delay what we can do today for tomorrow.

On tough days when self-love feels hard, I remember that the same Creator who made the sun, moon, stars, butterflies, sea creatures, and my loved ones also made me.

Believing we are created as perfectly as any part of the universe encourages us to shine our light.

It's a reminder that our transformation journey isn't finished; it's a reassurance that we are enough. It's a reminder that God has already gone ahead of us to clear the path.

We don't need to be perfect or to be a different version of ourselves. We just have to show up, knowing who we are, where we are in our journey, what we think, what we have to say, and how we can serve — it's enough. God is the provider. We are the vessel.

Loving Kindness

Journal Entry, May 31, 2020

Today's meditation was difficult. I felt compelled to acknowledge the current events unfolding in the world following the death of George Floyd. I practiced a loving kindness meditation and read from Cleo Wade's book *Where to Begin*. I am re-listening to it now, and I still feel emotional. My heart aches and hurts for the violence, the pain, the suffering, and the desperation.

While reading the Cleo Wade book, I came across this passage that I had written when I first read it.

I am unlearning lessons and behaviors that don't serve me. These lessons conditioned me to play small, hoping for a pat on the head, recognition, or reward to prove I was good enough. I never felt good enough. There were always others who were smarter, prettier, thinner, more talented, with the right background, who knew the rules, had a better vocabulary, more money, or more supportive parents, and so on.

I have lived as separate identities since I moved to the States, trying to figure out who to be with my family and my community to be "perfect" and "good," and how to be the American version of what would guarantee "success." I am always striving, working harder, and trying to please. I fear being called out for not belonging, for being a fraud, or for not being good enough. I did not stand in my power and instead resented myself for it. I needed control but also sought comfort, love, and someone to take care of me so I could catch my breath and relax, even if just for a few minutes.

I fluctuated between self-care and self-harm. I stopped looking after myself, my health, and everything else in pursuit of external validation. I pushed myself too hard and nearly destroyed myself and those I loved most. Then, I finally said enough. I am DONE.

I stepped off the carousel in the middle of the ride, and as I looked back at it, I felt such peace and gratitude that I finally had the courage to step out in faith and say "no." I softly sank into God's open arms. "I've been waiting for you," He told me.

So, I began a new chapter of self-love, self-discovery, and self-acceptance. As I shed the heavy layers I'd been wearing, I realized I no longer needed them. I am lighter, freer, happier, more grateful, and joyful.

I am more myself than ever before. My passions have been unleashed, and I embrace them fully. Now, I will prioritize those that bring the most value to others. There is time to explore purposefully. They will not go away. I am focused, clear, and overwhelmed with gratitude for the blessings in my life. I choose to believe in God's promises. If we can imagine it, He can bring it to pass. So, with prayer, I ask Him to show me daily the three things I need to do to stay on the right path. I practice peace, love, hope, joy, gratitude, and courage daily for myself, my family, and the world around me. I will ask, "How can I help?" I will partner with others to grow and learn. I trust that there is always enough.

Your Divine Purpose Practices

How can you fully embrace your identity as God's handiwork and step into the purpose He has prepared for you? These practices will guide you in discovering how to shine your light more brightly, physically experience what it feels like to trust God's plan, and assess specific areas where you might still be trying to earn your worth through achievement. You don't need to qualify yourself; you're already qualified by the Creator who designed you as His masterpiece.

1. Journal Prompt

How can you make your light shine brighter in the world?

What good works do you feel called to do in the world?

How can you be more confident that God has already paved the way for you?

2. Embodiment Practice: Stepping into Purpose

Find a quiet spot where you can sit comfortably, close your eyes, and focus on your breathing.

Bring to mind a calling or purpose that you believe God has placed in your heart. Visualize yourself stepping into that purpose and taking action. Imagine yourself doing God's work in the world. How do you feel?

Imagine yourself growing more confident and empowered as you see God ahead of you, lighting your path and paving the way. How can you step into your purpose?

This verse urges us to find peace in our identity as God's creation. You are God's living masterpiece, intentionally crafted to reflect His creative beauty in ways nobody else can.

This doesn't mean you will never improve or grow; instead, your development comes from a place of security rather than from striving. You don't need to earn your place in God's story—you already have one. Your role isn't to qualify yourself but to trust the One who has already qualified you.

Your journey of purpose awaits. Will you step into the good works God has prepared for you today?

Chapter 13
Talent Multiplication

The Parable of the Talents (Matthew 25:14-30)

At that time, God's kingdom will be like a man leaving home to travel to another place for a visit. Before he left, he talked with his servants. He told his servants to take care of his belongings while he was away. He decided how much each servant would be able to care for.

The man gave one servant five bags of money. He gave another servant two bags. And he gave a third servant one bag. Then he left.

The servant who got five bags went quickly to invest the money. Those five bags of money earned five more. It was the same with the servant who had two bags. That servant invested the money and earned two more. But the servant who got one bag of money went away and dug a hole in the ground. Then he hid his master's money in the hole.

After a long time, the master came home. He asked the servants what they did with his money. The servant who got five bags brought that amount and five more bags of money to the master. The servant said, "Master, you trusted me to care for five bags of money. So, I used them to earn five more."

The master answered, "You did right. You are a good servant who can be trusted. You did well with that small amount of money. So, I will let you care for much greater things. Come and share my happiness with me."

Then, the servant who received two bags of money came to the master. The servant said, "Master, you gave me two bags of money to care for. So, I used your two bags to earn two more."

The master replied, "You did the right thing. You're a trustworthy servant. You handled a small amount of money well. Therefore, I will entrust you with greater responsibilities. Come and share my happiness with me."

Then, the servant who received one bag of money came to the master. The servant said, "Master, I knew you were a very hard man. You harvest what you did not plant. You gather crops where you did not put any seed. So, I was afraid. I went and hid your money in the ground. Here is the one bag of money you gave me."

The master answered, "You are a bad and lazy servant! You say you knew that I harvest what I did not plant and that I gather crops where I did not put any seed. So, you should have put my money in the bank. Then, when I came home, I would get my money back. And I would also get the interest that my money earned."

So, the master told his other servants, "Take the one bag of money from that servant and give it to the servant who has ten bags. Everyone who uses what they have will get more. They will have much more than they need. But people who do not use what they have will have everything taken away from them." Then the master said, "Throw that useless servant outside into the darkness, where people will cry and grind their teeth with pain."

The Courage to Invest What We've Been Given

This passage used to confuse and scare me. When I first read the Parable of the Talents, I felt pulled in different directions. I was inspired by the servants who multiplied their gifts, but I also felt deeply uneasy with the master's harsh response to the fearful servant who thought that saving was better.

I see talent as both a source of actual income and a symbol of the gifts God has given us all. The entire master-servant relationship made me feel uneasy. I wondered, "Is this really how God operates? Through fear and punishment?" It didn't align with the compassionate God that I know and love.

However, over time, my understanding shifted from just analyzing it with my mind to letting it work on my heart. I began to see the deeper message underneath. What if this isn't about judgment at all, but about the heartbreak of wasted potential? What if the master's disappointment wasn't anger but genuine sorrow over what could have been? What gifts are we—am I—burying out of fear when they were meant to grow and multiply?

Once I looked beyond my human filters and understanding, the lesson became clear. This story isn't asking me to be perfect — it's inviting me to be faithful with what I've been given, trusting that even my imperfect efforts can multiply when placed in God's hands.

Divine Investment

During this time, a talent represented a large amount of money or wealth. The Master, in this context, can be seen as God, and we are His servants. Jesus shared this parable with His disciples because He knew that His time on Earth was ending, and He was preparing them for His return to heaven.

Although the currency in this parable is made up of talents of silver or gold, the metaphor applies to our lives today. Each of us has something valuable entrusted to us. This lesson highlights our duty to be good stewards of what we've been given. Similar to the servants in the Parable of the Talents, the apostles each received their message about what was expected of them after Jesus's crucifixion.

As humans, created in the image of God, we each receive talents, gifts, experiences, and discernment to use throughout our lives. We are unique; our gifts differ, and our purpose varies. Our role isn't to compare what we've been given with others, but to multiply what we already have to create more blessings, talents, impact, and legacy. We're called to develop and enhance our skills. We shouldn't waste what we've been given, but instead use it to expand for the better.

Stewardship Not Ownership

What has been given to me is not meant to be hoarded or buried in the ground; it has been given to circulate and multiply. I am here to do my best with what I've been given, using my natural gifts and talents, and investing in others. I do this when I support someone who teaches me something so I can be a blessing to someone else.

There's a certain heaviness that comes with burying our gifts under the weight of "what might have been." But there's also an unmistakable lightness that appears when we start to invest faithfully in what we've been given, even if imperfectly.

My job isn't to compare what others have received and wish it were mine. There are eight billion people on the planet; no two individuals are exactly the same, and no two have experienced the same combination of talents. I celebrate what others are doing and seek inspiration from them because no one can help all eight billion people except God. And He does that through each of us—if we each do our part.

Finding Your Measure

This parable teaches us that the goal wasn't for the servant with two talents to match the servant with five, but to make good use of what he had. When we invest our time, resources, gifts, and money and don't bury them, we create and grow what we've been given.

I've thought about what I've hidden in my life. For years, I mostly kept my spiritual insights to myself, worried about judgment and criticism. I felt called to write, speak, and teach about spiritual growth, but I kept it quiet, focusing instead on what seemed safer and more acceptable. Like the third servant, I acted out of fear rather than faith.

The turning point was when I realized that my gifts weren't truly mine to keep. They were given to me to use and leverage, not to hide away. This realization changed everything. If these talents really come from God, then hiding them isn't humility; it's disobedience. And if they are meant to serve others, keeping them secret isn't protecting myself; it's withholding something that could help someone else on their journey.

Fear of Judgement

Journal Entry, October 25, 2022

I've been holding back because I'm afraid of being seen, judged, or making mistakes. But what if my fear is actually selfishness in disguise? What if someone needs exactly what I have to offer, and I'm keeping it from them because I'm too scared to put myself out there? God didn't give me these gifts so I could perfect them before using them. He gave them to me to use imperfectly while trusting Him with the outcome.

Okay, thank you, God, for once again showing me how you have already shared everything in your Word if we have eyes to see and ears to hear.

I live each day doing what I need to do. God is taking care of the rest. He has, is, and will support me completely. His ways are not our ways—they are better if we get out of His way.

I believe God has already fully equipped me with everything I need to do my part. In His timing, everything will be revealed as it should be.

That morning changed my view of my talents. I started sharing more openly, taking bigger risks, and investing what I had instead of waiting until I felt "ready" or "worthy" enough to use it. And just as the parable promises, I've seen those talents grow, not because I'm exceptionally skilled, but because that's what happens when we faithfully invest what we've been given.

Don't hide or neglect your talents and gifts, or they could be taken away. Avoid comparing what you've been given to others, since they have their own mission, purpose, and gifts to share with the world. Do what you can with what you've been entrusted with, and it will be blessed and multiplied.

When Crisis Reveals Opportunity

I saw this happen during COVID. When the pandemic hit, everyone's business changed overnight. While others scrambled to adapt, I noticed something different happening in my own life. My personal meditation practice and daily routines helped me not just survive, but I also felt pretty good, while I watched others struggle. I found myself centered and clear, which led me to ask: "How can I serve?"

I decided to offer two free services: morning meditation sessions and lunch-and-learn workshops for organizations. Most organizations I approached said "yes" to the idea of a free workshop aimed at empowering their employees with practical tools for handling the challenges of shutdown and remote work.

What I received in return was gratitude for the impact I made. What I didn't expect was that many of those same organizations contacted me again in Q3 to develop more workshops for their teams. This became a new part of my business where I could add value to more people, share content I was passionate about, and in turn, grow my business. By investing my talent, God multiplied it.

And that morning meditation group that was supposed to be temporary? I ended up leading it six days a week for five years, creating a community of support and spiritual growth that lasted well beyond the initial crisis. All because I chose to invest in what I had been given instead of ignoring it.

What started as a simple service offering evolved into a new aspect of my business where I could serve more people, share content I care about, and grow my work at the same time. By investing the talents I had been given— my meditation practice, facilitation skills, and understanding of wellbeing— God expanded them in ways I could never have planned on my own.

The Abundance of Shared Gifts

What I love about The Parable of the Talents is how the master didn't just ask the servants to return what they had been given; instead, he invited them to create more, not only for themselves but for the greater good. When we invest our talents faithfully, we create ripples that extend well beyond us. Your voice might be exactly what someone needs to hear to find their courage. Your creativity could inspire people you'll never even meet. Your compassion might be the saving grace in someone's darkest hour.

This is how faithful stewardship works. We each invest what we've been given, and together, there's more than enough. We become lanterns of light in a world that needs us to show up.

The Freedom in Faithful Stewardship

This means we can relax from the pressure to perform and compare. Our job isn't to achieve specific results but to faithfully manage what we've been entrusted with—whether that's five talents, two, or one. The outcome is in God's hands.

Once we understand this, we free ourselves to take risks, try new things, and step out in faith instead of waiting until we feel fully qualified or fully prepared. Growth happens by investing, not by hiding.

What talent is God asking you to discover today? What gift have you been hesitant to share? What dream have you buried out of fear? It's never too late to start investing in what you've been given. God values faithfulness more than perfection.

Your Talent Practices

I've created these practices to help you recognize and develop the unique talents God has given you. These practices will guide you in evaluating how you're currently using your gifts, allow you to physically experience the shift from fear to faithful action, and help you identify specific areas where you might be hiding talents meant to flourish. God isn't asking for perfection; He's inviting you to faithfully invest whatever He has entrusted to you, trusting that even your imperfect efforts can multiply in His hands.

1. Journal Prompt

What have you done with the talents and gifts you've been given?

How have you multiplied them to benefit others?

What's stopping you from maximizing their potential?

2. Embodiment Exercise: Moving from Fear to Action

Sit quietly, close your eyes, and concentrate on your breath.

Visualize the gifts and talents that God has given you and imagine yourself using them to their fullest in the world. Feel your confidence grow with every step you take.

Take proactive steps with your gifts and imagine yourself making a positive impact in the world. How does it feel to step forward in faith with what God has given you?

The Parable of the Talents reminds us that we are not owners but stewards of what God has entrusted to us. Everything we have comes from Him and is meant to be invested for the greater good.

This doesn't mean we all need to achieve the same results. God doesn't compare us to others but asks if we've been faithful with our individual responsibilities.

Maybe the most important lesson is that the fear of failure, judgment, or inadequacy often causes us to hide our talents instead of risking their use. But God calls us to step outside our comfort zones in faith, trusting that He who gave the gifts will also bring growth when we faithfully invest them.

Your journey of multiplication awaits. How will you let your light shine today?

Chapter 14

Your Way, Not Mine

"'Lord, what about this man?' Jesus said to him, 'If it is my will that he remain until I come, what is that to you? You follow me!'"
–John 21:21–22

Do you ever compare yourself to others, coveting their success or wondering when you'll be further along in your journey toward your goals? Honestly, it's difficult not to compare myself to others, especially as an entrepreneur. It's hard not to look at what others are doing or see the results they're achieving. So, this is a story I revisit when I catch myself comparing myself to others or worrying about what they're doing. It reminds me to focus on myself instead.

The Comparing Heart

After the resurrection, Jesus walked with Peter and asked him if he loved Him. Peter replied that he did. Then Jesus told Peter that from then on, he would be caring for Jesus's sheep. He had been chosen to grow the church, share the gospel, and be willing to die for his faith. Jesus emphasized the importance of Peter's role. He would be a leader and a pillar. Peter seemed to be listening, and then, when he saw the apostle John, he asked Jesus, "Lord, what about this man?" Instead of focusing on his mission, he was curious about what Jesus had planned for John.

Peter is like us—so human, so devout, yet so flawed. Don't we do the same? Haven't I repeated this pattern? Instead of listening to what God wants us to do, we focus on the external world. Instead of following His guidance for our lives, purposes, and businesses, we look at what others are doing and ask, "Why not me?"

This is human nature, and I think of Peter whenever I catch myself doing the same thing. Although he and John were both following Jesus, both disciples, and both had personal relationships with Jesus, Peter still wondered about someone else's mission instead of focusing on his own.

Finding My Own Path

Journal Entry, January 31, 2025

I recently joined another business group and became part of a larger community of entrepreneurs around the world. Everyone has a different business; mine is one of the smallest, or at least it feels that way. I often notice how others have more social media followers, bigger email lists, higher revenue, larger teams, and so on. My mind struggles. I feel inferior, as if I'm not in the right place and should be further along. I wanted to be a small fish in a big pond, but feeling this way isn't always inspiring; it can also be limiting. Then I remembered this verse.

My job isn't to compare myself to others. My job is to stay connected to God so I can listen to His will for me, my life, and my business. Staying aligned with God's will ensures my business is blessed. It also helps me use my gifts and talents for the highest good of all. Being aligned means I am grateful and content with what God has planned for me, and I don't try to manipulate, fight against, or bargain with God about what I want.

This is my daily practice of surrender. I catch myself being like Peter and turning back to God.

Can I be grateful for where I am? Can I be content with what I have? Can I trust that God's plans are greater than my own?

Divine Obedience

I'm at a point where I question my plans, dreams, and ambitions, wondering if they align with God's will. I don't want to act outside of God's will. I know with every fiber of my being that when I live in alignment, God's power flows through me in ways that can't be explained.

I was terrified when I heard God tell me to leave my job and start my own business. I never saw myself as an entrepreneur. I worried about money, getting clients, selling my services, not having a steady paycheck, making decisions on my own, pivoting, adjusting, creating constantly, and managing all the many tasks that a business owner faces. And yet, I listened and have been supported every step of the way.

I recognize that saying "yes" to the call was my act of obedience. God feeds me daily exactly what I need—nothing less, nothing more. Now, my act of obedience is to be patient, to trust, to let God stretch me in new ways, and to test my desire and capacity for more. My obedience means staying aligned with God's calling and mission for me. Not my will, but His.

I thank God that He constantly shows me that even the disciples who followed the living, breathing Jesus still struggled because, as humans, we do too. If they had been perfect, I would feel shame when I struggle. However, since we have Peter as an example—both a pillar of the church and a deeply human, flawed person—I am encouraged that God can use me as well.

Your Unique Purpose Practices

I've developed these practices to help you let go of comparison and embrace your unique divine journey. They will guide you in understanding how comparison has affected your peace, help you experience the freedom that comes from releasing envy, and evaluate specific areas where you might be distracted by others' paths instead of focusing on your own. Remember, Jesus isn't asking you to follow someone else's way—He's inviting you to follow Him in the special way He has called you.

1. Journal Prompt

Do you compare your journey to someone else's? Whose and why?

How has this impacted your peace?

What would it mean to fully trust God's plan for your life?

2. Embodiment Exercise: Releasing Comparison

Find a quiet spot to sit, close your eyes, and focus on your breath. Ground yourself and relax.

Consider a time when you compared yourself to someone else or wished for what another person had.

What feelings does that bring up?

Now, picture yourself surrendering those emotions to God. Feel Him remove any resentment, jealousy, pain, or insecurity.

Now imagine fully embracing your purpose and trusting God to guide and support you. What does that feel like?

Jesus's question to Peter reminds us of a deep truth: each of us has a unique journey with God. When we fixate on others' paths—their successes, gifts, and callings—we shift our focus away from the sacred work God has specifically given us.

This doesn't mean we can't learn from or be inspired by others. However, it does mean that our focus should be on faithfully following Jesus in the way He has called each of us personally. Your path won't look like anyone else's because that's not the way it was meant to be. The gifts, challenges, timing, and purpose God has for you are uniquely yours.

We don't need to understand or approve of God's plans for others; we just need to trust and follow His plans for us. When Peter asked about John, Jesus basically said, "That's between John and me—your job is to follow where I'm leading you."

Your unique journey of purpose awaits. Will you keep your eyes fixed on Jesus today rather than looking at others?

Chapter 15
Working Together for Good

"And we know that all things work together for good to them that love God, to them who are called according to his purpose."
–Romans 8:28

When I struggle with trying to control situations or want to see how things will turn out, I remember this verse. Still, my control issues persist despite all my best intentions. It's easy to forget how powerful our God is when our problems feel overwhelming. As we go through life, we don't always know if everything will turn out okay. We can't see into the future before taking leaps of faith. That's why they are called leaps of faith. God's timing often doesn't match ours. We want quick results, clear paths, and immediate changes, but divine timing works differently.

A Promise of Purpose

Paul wrote this verse to the church in Rome. It was directed to early Christians who were both Jewish and Gentile. They came from diverse backgrounds and traditions and were now seeking ways to live their faith and embrace the promises Jesus offered. Paul encouraged these believers to have faith and courage, even when they felt uncertain and scared. He wanted to give them hope that their lives had meaning and purpose, and that even in confusion or suffering, God was working all circumstances together for their good.

The Beginning of My Journey

Journal Entry, November 18, 2018

I resigned from my job a few weeks ago. It won't be announced for several days, but I already know. I started and finished re-reading *The Alchemist*. I've read it multiple times, usually every year. It's a short book that can be read in one sitting, which is how I've read it before. I usually read it for the story, often rushing through without taking time to reflect on its meaning. I began rereading the book yesterday and finished it this morning. This time, it resonated with me more deeply because of the journey I've been on.

Having decided to follow my dreams, I am leaving the comfort of a stable job and paycheck for the unknown. Even though it's scary, I know I have to do this. My readings have focused on recognizing my fear, surrendering it to the Holy Spirit, and taking action despite my hesitation. The other message has been to trust that everything will work out. "And we know that all things work together for good to them that love God, to them who are called according to his purpose" (Romans 8:28). "And, when you want something, all the universe conspires in helping you to achieve it." –The Alchemist.

I do have fears. For many years, I've prioritized comfort and security over following my heart's desires. I've spent ordinary days filled with moments of joy, love, and passion from my family and friends because it was easier and because that's what those close to me were doing, too.

This reminds me of the biggest lie in *The Alchemist*. The main character, Santiago, a shepherd boy, meets the old man Melchizedek, the King of Salem. Santiago sits on a stone bench, feeling troubled and torn between the simple life he's familiar with and the irresistible pull of a dream he can't ignore.

An old man approached him and, without any introduction, sat down beside him. Santiago listened as the old man spoke of "Personal Legends," the purpose every soul is meant to fulfill. Then, the old man leaned in closer, his voice dropping to a whisper as if revealing a secret of the universe itself.

At some point in our lives, we lose control of what happens to us, and fate takes charge of our lives. That's the world's greatest lie.

Santiago asks him what a Personal Legend is, and the old man explains that it is what we are here to achieve— the dream that the Soul of the World has placed in our hearts.

He tells Santiago that everyone knows their Personal Legend when they are young, but over time, fear, routine, and the belief in the "world's greatest lie" cause most people to abandon it.

I bought into that lie. I tried to hide my dreams of writing a book, teaching at a university, traveling around the world to speak, and sharing what I've learned on my life's journey. I was afraid to say these things out loud, worried people would laugh or think I was arrogant. Who was I to have such big dreams? "Who do you think you are?"

"Our deepest fear is not that we are inadequate. Our deepest fear is that we are powerful beyond measure. It is our light, not our darkness, that most frightens us. We ask ourselves, 'Who am I to be brilliant, gorgeous, talented, fabulous?' Actually, who are you not to be? You are a child of God. Your playing small does not serve the world. There is nothing enlightened about shrinking so that other people won't feel insecure around you. We are all meant to shine, as children do. We were born to manifest the glory of God that is within us. It's not just in some of us; it's in everyone. And as we let our own light shine, we unconsciously give other people permission to do the same. As we are liberated from our own fear, our presence automatically liberates others."

–Marianne Williamson

This quote by Marianne Williamson has fascinated me since the first time I read it. I don't remember exactly when I first read it, but I was so struck by it that I printed it out and hung it on my office wall. I kept revisiting it, questioning whether I truly believed the words. Does she mean me? Does Williamson really believe that each of us is here to play big and serve the world? Do I have permission to let my light shine? Could I genuinely be "fabulous"? Do I have the courage to live my truth?

While contemplating and reading this quote daily at work, the irony is that I wasn't living a life where I felt powerful, light, brilliant, gorgeous, talented, or fabulous. It would sometimes take me two hours to get out the door in the morning. I needed to read three Scripture books, a chapter in another self-help book, journal, pray, do yoga, and meditate before jumping in the shower. Yes, I know there is a problem if I need so much reinforcement to motivate myself to work in the morning.

Just typing these words makes me feel guilty. I know I am blessed beyond measure and often kneel, thanking God daily for my wonderful husband, daughters, family, and friends. The Lord has provided for our needs, and that recognition has become my excuse for not asking for more. "Who am I to ask for more?" I wonder.

I convinced myself I should be grateful for my corporate career. I started my career many years ago at a company where I was given opportunities to take on more responsibilities, work in different areas, and develop my leadership skills. My job provided financial stability. However, I never felt like I was being true to myself. I reached a point where I didn't recognize or like who I was anymore, my health started to decline, and my old friends from college stopped asking about the dreams I used to share with them. I felt stuck.

I long to reconnect with my true self. What happened to the passionate young writer? What happened to my younger self, who was confident and comfortable in her own skin? My girls are grown, and I wonder if they know who I am or what dreams I still hold for my life. Now, I've started a journey of self-discovery again, living mindfully in the present, without expectations, and finding joy in the here and now. I plan to let the next chapter of my life unfold, trusting that God is guiding me.

Living in Trust

I am so grateful that everything works together for those who are called to His purpose. Today, I wake up knowing I am on my path, and every day, I trust that more synchronicities occur, more doors open, and more blessings flow to me because I am living my dharma.

I wake up each day feeling a pleasant hum. I believe it's my vibration and frequency. I trust that as I grow stronger, the work I do will provide more value, attract more clients, and ultimately lead to financial abundance. I have planted many seeds and am patiently waiting for God to bring a wave of ongoing financial blessings. I asked, I believed, and I received.

There were times when I wondered why certain doors didn't open and why opportunities I thought were perfect didn't happen. Looking back, I see that those delays and redirections were protections—God was clearing the way for something better, and more in line with my true purpose.

The scripture doesn't promise that all things are good. It promises that all things work together for good. That "working together" part is crucial. It implies a process, a divine weaving of circumstances that creates something beautiful out of even the most challenging situations.

Finding Purpose in Pain

Some of my greatest growth has come from my most painful experiences. The heartbreaks, failures, and disappointments have shaped me in ways that success alone never could. When I trust that God is working all things together for my good, I can endure even the hardest seasons.

What is God preparing me for through this challenge? How is this helping me get ready for what I will need in the next chapter? What limiting beliefs is this situation revealing that I need to release?

We will face storms, but each one serves a purpose in the hands of a loving God who is dedicated to our growth and well-being.

Trust as a Daily Practice

Trusting that all things work together for good is a daily practice. Some mornings I wake up and immediately feel that alignment, that sense that I'm exactly where I'm supposed to be. Other days, doubt creeps in, and I have to choose trust over fear intentionally.

On difficult days, I find that focusing on gratitude helps me regain perspective. When I think about how God has worked in my life—how doors that once seemed permanently closed suddenly opened, how relationships that appeared broken were restored, and how ideas that once seemed impossible became reality—my faith is renewed again and again.

Trust is discovering peace even amid uncertainty. It's understanding that the God who has brought you this far will not abandon you now.

Your Divine Trust Practices

I've designed these practices to help you build trust in God's perfect timing. They will guide you in recognizing what might be holding you back from your purpose, experiencing the shift from anxiety to peace when you surrender control, and identifying specific areas where you might be resisting divine timing. Remember, God isn't asking you to understand the entire journey— He's inviting you to trust that He's working everything together for your good, even when the process feels uncertain.

1. Journal Prompt

Are you fulfilling your purpose? What's stopping you?

What would it feel like to surrender to God and trust that everything will unfold in His perfect timing?

2. Embodiment Practice: Trusting the Process

Sit or stand comfortably, close your eyes, take a few deep breaths, and relax your body.

Now, imagine a moment when you faced a tough situation and weren't sure how it would turn out. Feel the emotions you went through—maybe uncertainty, fear, or frustration.

Now, picture viewing that situation through faith, knowing that God is working everything together for your good. Embrace the peace and confidence that come from understanding that God is in control. As you breathe deeply, say aloud, "I trust that God is working all things together for my good. I may not understand the process, but I trust His purpose."

Open your eyes and reflect on how it feels to let go of control and trust in God's plan. What shifts in your heart and mind when you embrace the idea that everything—good and bad—is part of His greater plan for you?

This promise from Romans doesn't mean that everything that happens to us is good; I know that there is suffering and pain in our world that breaks God's heart. I believe it means that God can work through all circumstances—even painful ones—to ultimately bring about something good for those who love Him and live according to His purpose.

The key is to see our lives through a divine perspective instead of just focusing on our immediate circumstances. When we trust that God is working everything together for good, we gain the courage to take risks, follow our calling, and embrace the fullness of who we were meant to be.

Will you believe today that God is working all things—even the difficult things—together for your good?

DIVINE PROVISION

Chapter 16

Ask, Believe, Receive

*"Therefore, I tell you, whatever you ask for in prayer, believe that you have
received it, and it will be yours." –Mark 11:24 NIV*

I was sitting at my desk one morning, looking at a list of dreams that felt
impossibly far away. A book I wanted to write. A retreat I longed to host in
Tuscany. A coaching practice that would impact lives around the world. As I
read my goals and hopes, a whisper reminded me of Jesus's words: *"Whatever
you ask for in prayer, believe that you have received it, and it will be yours."*

There are many verses in the Bible that tell us to believe before we see, to trust
without proof or physical evidence. In this teaching, Jesus presents a powerful
spiritual formula: ask, believe, receive. Not "ask, receive, then believe" or even
"ask, wait anxiously, and maybe receive if you're lucky." The important
middle step—belief—is the crucial link between asking and receiving.

The Prayer of Faith

In this verse, Jesus teaches His disciples how to pray effectively. He is not
describing a technique; He is revealing a spiritual principle about how divine
provision operates. Prayer is rooted in faith, trusting in God's power. It should
be done with strong confidence that God is listening and that He is not only
capable but willing to answer our prayers.

This kind of prayer is active rather than passive. Our beliefs and knowledge
are the keys that unlock receiving. Jesus tells us that belief comes before
receiving and that our faith activates the prayer. It's as if faith is the spiritual
currency that allows divine gifts to flow into our lives.

I've found myself stuck at different stages of this process at various times in
my spiritual journey. Sometimes, I stay in the asking phase, continuing to
petition without moving into belief. At other times, I jump straight to
receiving without taking the necessary intermediate step of cultivating deep,

embodied faith. And it's in the believing—that space of complete trust—where the real spiritual work happens.

The Power of Believing

Believing is the waiting; it's holding the vision, being patient, and knowing so profoundly in our soul that manifestation is on the way. But this isn't passive waiting—it's an active expectation charged with certainty.

It's not about our timing or will; it's about God's divine timing and His will. The lessons are found in waiting, surrendering, and taking time to rest and pause—things that don't come naturally to me. I often find myself constantly taking action. I have a lot of energy and love to create and make things happen. I tend to be impatient. Over time, I've learned that aligned action is the best approach; otherwise, it's just a list of tasks that aren't aimed at the right goals or dreams. It's like a beautifully wrapped present that's empty inside.

For years, I was stuck in the asking stage—praying to discover my purpose, asking God to improve my work situation, to see my calling clearly, and to ease the pain I was experiencing. I kept praying, journaling, and meditating on the same requests year after year, never taking the next vital step: believing.

It wasn't that I didn't believe in God or His power. I believed in God, the stories I read in the Bible, and His ability to work miracles. What I didn't believe was that He would answer my specific prayers. I feared disappointment, although I'd never admit it at the time. My faith wasn't internal or embodied—it was theoretical rather than experiential.

From Belief to Manifestation

Everything changed when I finally started to believe that my prayers had already been answered and that things were already moving forward; that divine provision was happening even if I couldn't see the evidence yet. I relaxed. I let go of my prayers and stopped holding onto them so tightly. I handed them over to God's care and timing.

Not only did I feel better and enjoy life more, but things also moved forward quickly after that shift in consciousness. It wasn't that God waited until I believed to start working — it was that my belief allowed me to participate in what He was already doing.

Tremendous Growth

Journal Entry, December 1, 2019

We are a few weeks away from the start of the New Year. This year has been a time of self-care, self-work, and self-reflection. 2019 became a year of travel, spending time alone, releasing fears and limiting beliefs, growth, and building a new foundation for the future. Every day, I learned something new, tried something I had never done before, and figured things out without the help of an assistant or team. I know that God and I are partnering now. I don't have a team to support me or a coach at the moment. My teachers are the many books I read, the podcasts I listened to, my daily spiritual practices, journals, and this laptop I'm typing on.

Thank goodness for the written word. I read past entries and sometimes cry at the progress I've made. I have made mistakes and relapsed into fear, but I have climbed my way out and stepped into faith. The flesh is weak, but the spirit is stronger when I discern what is real and what is not. We are not our thoughts. My dear friend Prem says in his book that our lives express the limit of our thoughts. That is so true! We often stop short of reaching our goals because we fear we won't be able to achieve them.

I started cutting out pictures to make a new vision board for 2020. The one for 2019 focused on balance, self-care, travel, affirmations, getting healthy, starting my business, and even building a pergola in my backyard. Not surprisingly, since I believe in the power of visual images turning into reality, many of the things on my board have already come true.

Instead of putting this board away, I am creating a new one to accompany it in 2020. I don't want to forget the intent and necessity of what I envisioned for my life in 2019. Balance, health, and treating myself well need to stay.

However, I feel a strong sense of urgency to accomplish my career goals in 2020. My work in 2019 has prepared me to become who I need to be to pursue my big, bold goals in 2020.

Without becoming a better version of myself, there can be no better future. I feel a strong sense of urgency and a burning desire to pursue my big dreams. There has been a noticeable shift in me. I used to think I understood God's promises, but now I feel my faith is deeply rooted within me. I BELIEVE His promises. Ask, believe, receive.

And I believe in His will. A few weeks ago, I took a step back, and God said "no" to the opportunity. For the first time in my life, I didn't spend much time wishing it had turned out differently. I approached the experience with the belief that if it's God's will, it will happen easily, and if it's not, He will make it clear that He has something better planned for me.

This journal entry reflects the shift in my spiritual understanding—moving from merely agreeing with God's promises intellectually to genuinely believing in their fulfillment in my life. It wasn't just positive thinking; it was faith coming alive inside me.

Aligned Action: Faith Made Visible

What I've also learned on my journey is the importance of taking action. I spent years waiting for God to do something and change my circumstances. Waiting for a new job, a new opportunity, and to be recognized for how amazing I am. I spent years waiting.

Then I stopped waiting and started taking action. I acted many times without knowing exactly what to do or how to do it. Still, I meditated and prayed every day to be shown the three best things to do that day to move forward in the right direction. That didn't seem impossible or overwhelming; it felt manageable.

I started my LLC, built a website, wrote content, began coaching, started consulting, planned and hosted a retreat in a foreign country I'd never been to, and I began blogging. I achieved many impressive things that had previously only been distant dreams.

It may seem like manifestation happens overnight, but it doesn't. Our faith and belief set everything into motion—that's the true catalyst, not just the prayer. The prayer represents the vision, while belief drives us into aligned action toward that vision. When I began to do my part, God accelerated everything, and it manifested quite quickly in my life. I often felt unable to keep up with the synchronicities and opportunities. I held on as opportunities appeared, and I responded.

For years, I wanted to organize a retreat in Tuscany. I could clearly picture the house in my mind, but I hesitated to take action. Then, one day, while browsing Airbnb, I found the villa. It was even more beautiful than I had imagined, and I instantly knew it was the perfect choice. Not only did I quickly fill the villa with retreat participants, but I also rented another house down the road because we had so many interested guests.

Writing my book was another example of this principle in action. Once I decided the book would be a daily meditation, I made a plan and started writing every day. Soon, I finished the book that had been an unrealized dream for so long.

Divine Partnership in Manifestation

When I read books on manifestation, especially the earlier ones, they are full of scripture because God has already explained how this process works. Ask, believe, receive. We are co-creating our lives with Him. But I don't think we get to skip steps.

If we have the vision and ask, we must believe it is possible and take aligned action in that direction—no matter how uncomfortable we feel. Once we take action, we need to be present and mindful to notice the synchronicities, blessings, and abundance around us. Things might not turn out exactly as we imagined, but they could be even better.

The formula Jesus gave us isn't a magic spell that absolves us from involvement. It's an invitation to partner with the divine.

1. Ask - Express your desires and needs to God with clarity and authenticity.

2. Believe - Cultivate unwavering faith that what you've asked for is already in process.

3. Act - Take inspired steps that align with your prayer and demonstrate your belief.

4. Receive - Stay open, attentive, and grateful to recognize and accept divine provision.

We miss the fullness of this spiritual principle when we view it as a passive process or try to control every detail ourselves. True co-creation with God happens in that sacred middle ground between surrender and action, between trusting and participating.

Your Ask-Believe-Receive Practices

I've designed these practices to help you move from simply asking to truly believing and receiving. They will guide you in identifying clear next steps toward your prayer, help you physically experience what it feels like to embody the confidence of answered prayer, and honestly assess your current stance in the spiritual process regarding each of your desires. Remember, God isn't asking you to wait passively; He's inviting you into a divine partnership where your belief acts as the bridge between asking and receiving.

1. Journal Prompt

Reflect on your current desire or request for your life. Ask to be shown the three next best steps you can take today to move in the right direction. Write these down, along with how you will recognize when God has answered this prayer.

2. Embodiment Exercise: Aligning Your Belief with Your Prayer

Sit or stand comfortably, close your eyes, and take a few deep breaths.

Picture what you're praying for. Visualize how it appears if your request has already been granted. Experience the emotions that come with receiving it.

As you take a deep breath, tell yourself: "I believe that what I have asked for in prayer is already mine. I trust in God's perfect timing and His faithfulness to me." Then, stretch your arms wide as if you're ready to receive.

Open your eyes and consider how you feel. How does this shift your mindset and perspective on the prayer you've offered?

Jesus's words in Mark 11:24 weren't just instructions for getting what we want; they were an invitation to a deeper understanding of how divine provision flows through human faith. When we align our expectations with God's promises and believe before we see evidence, we participate in the sacred dance of co-creation with the divine.

Will you move beyond asking into the powerful space of believing today?

Chapter 17
God's Plans to Prosper

"For I know the plans I have for you," declares the Lord, "plans to prosper you and not to harm you, plans to give you hope and a future." –Jeremiah 29:11

This might be the first verse I ever memorized, or perhaps the one I've turned to repeatedly when I felt anxious, worried, or uncertain about my future. I've clung to these words through every major transition in my life. I remember thinking of this verse as I drove alone on a four-hour trip back to my parents' house after graduation, with my car packed with everything I owned, and my mind filled with uncertainty about what lay ahead. No job lined up. No clear direction. Just the vast expanse of "real life" looming before me. In that moment of change, this promise became my lifeline.

It's easy to believe in God and praise Him when things go our way. However, it becomes harder to hold onto that belief when our circumstances are complicated and challenging. Losing faith or questioning whether God has forgotten us can seem natural when the path ahead is unclear, or when the doors we hoped would open stay firmly shut.

Words for Exiles

God spoke these words to the prophet Jeremiah during the seventh to sixth century BC. Jeremiah was writing to the exiled people of Judah living in Babylon. They had been taken captive after the destruction of Jerusalem and the temple. Their homeland was in ruins, their sacred spaces desecrated, and their future seemed hopeless.

Think about the exiled Israelites. Their homeland was lost, Jerusalem and the temple had been destroyed, and everything they identified with had disappeared. Their routines and religious practices were gone. Their daily lives had completely changed. They were suffering greatly, and God sent Jeremiah to give them hope. He didn't promise their pain would go away immediately, but He did promise that their current suffering was not the end of their story.

God was sending them hope and His promise that He would bring them back and provide for them. Even though their circumstances were difficult, He was working behind the scenes to prepare them for a brighter future. He was giving them hope for what they couldn't see.

This message is very important. These weren't words spoken to people in comfortable situations; they were lifelines given to those who felt abandoned and forgotten. The promise wasn't that they would never face hardship, but that hardship wouldn't be their final chapter.

A Life Without a Map

I graduated from college in 1994, before the internet, email, smartphones, or social media existed. My housemates and I stayed an extra week after graduation to spend time together after finals and enjoy our remaining moments before going home to start our adult lives.

After a week of living in Oxford, Ohio, I realized it was time to leave. The town felt different without all the college students, and since school was over, we had no real reason to stay—except that we wanted to delay "real life" a little longer.

I remember driving home the day we all left, and the four-hour drive to my parents' house felt incredibly long. Life was simpler then; we didn't have Sirius radio, Spotify, podcasts, or audiobooks to distract us. The ride was just me and my thoughts, except when I managed to catch a radio station I liked.

I didn't know what I was going to do next. Up to that point, everything was set. I didn't have a job lined up for after graduation or plans to move to another city like my housemates. I don't remember why I didn't have a plan for the next steps. I had only planned a backpacking trip across Europe with my friend Anne. I wanted to do that desperately and hoped I'd gain clarity on the trip.

The Unscripted Journey

What happened next in my life couldn't have been planned or predicted. When I got home, I found a job through a referral from Anne's mom over breakfast at their summer house in Illoud, France. The day I returned from that trip, I met Dorel, whom I would get engaged to four months later and marry a year after that.

The company I worked for had offices in New York, and I was able to transfer there easily before our wedding. After a few years in NY, Dorel and I decided to move to Cleveland and start our family where I grew up. We wanted to raise our children in the suburbs, in a house, take a bus to school, attend football games on Friday nights, and be close to my parents and sister.

When we moved, I left my job in New York City and became unemployed. I thought I'd eventually figure things out. While looking for another opportunity, I took a telemarketing job that I didn't particularly enjoy. My friend Marinika, a recruiter at KeyBank, suggested I interview for a retail associate position. I started that job less than two months after arriving in Cleveland and stayed there for twenty-two years.

Looking back, I see God's hand in everything. Getting a job over breakfast in France, meeting my husband the day I arrived home, my friend suggesting I apply at KeyBank—these weren't just coincidences. God was weaving my story together in ways I couldn't understand at the time. I just had to trust and take the next step. What seemed like coincidences from my limited view were, in fact, divine appointments from God's eternal perspective.

When I left my corporate career to start my own business, I had a vision of what it would look like, but I didn't have a detailed business plan. I returned to this verse, as I had many times before, believing that God had plans for me: to prosper me, not to harm me, and to give me hope and a future.

I have this quote from Scripture on my meditation altar in my office. I see it and read it every morning as I meditate. I can see it from my desk. It's a reminder that although I may not have everything in my life figured out, my creator has a better view and bigger plans. The times of greatest growth in my life were when I took risks and trusted in God.

Prosperity Beyond Material Wealth

When we read that God has "plans to prosper you," it's important to understand this in its fullest sense. The Hebrew word used here, "shalom," encompasses far more than financial success or material abundance. It signifies wholeness, completeness, and well-being in every dimension— physical, emotional, relational, and spiritual.

God's prosperity includes peace that transcends circumstances, purpose that aligns with divine intention, and provision that meets our deepest needs. It's not about exemption from difficulty but about sufficiency through it. It's not about acquiring more but about becoming more—more whole, more aligned, more of the person God created us to be.

Journal Entry, November 25, 2020

For the first time in my life, if my spirit were to leave this body, I would feel good about being a daughter, sister, wife, mother, friend, and human being. I have done more healing in the past two years than I have ever done before. I am finally serving, creating, and helping others as I always imagined I should. I didn't know how it would unfold when I was younger, but I always hoped that I would figure it out.

I reflect on my life, and I am grateful that You have protected me, God, guided me, directed my ways, and kept me where I needed to learn my lessons, grow, mold, and prepare myself. You have equipped me for Your plans for my life. I continue to listen carefully, to be guided, ready, and prepared to do Your work. I don't want to leave this body anytime soon. I still have many things to do. I have books inside me waiting to be written. I have retreats to create and facilitate. I have speeches to give. I have classes to teach. I have clients to help. I have lessons to learn. I have places to visit. I have people to meet, connect with, and grow alongside. I have philanthropic endeavors to join or align with. I still have meaningful work to do in this world.

I trust that if these dreams align with God's will for my life, they will come to fruition in ways I could never have imagined. His plans are always greater, better, and more aligned than my own.

This reflection reveals a shift in my perspective on prosperity—moving from accumulation to alignment, from achievement to purpose. True prosperity isn't about what we own but how fully we live out our divine calling.

The Sacred Pause

One of the most valuable lessons I've learned about God's plans is the importance of the waiting period—the sacred pause between chapters when nothing seems to be happening, yet everything is being prepared.

Before embarking on growth and quantum leaps into new adventures and experiences, I often feel a period of restlessness, uncertainty, and even a bit of discomfort. I've learned to pause and stay still during this time rather than rushing into action because something significant is on the horizon.

I feel that now, and I'm here for it.

These periods of restlessness and uncertainty aren't signs of God's absence but of His unseen work. Just as a seed must germinate in darkness before breaking through the soil into light, our next season often requires hidden preparation that we can't recognize until later.

The Israelites spent seventy years in exile before returning to their homeland. Joseph endured years in prison before his dreams were realized. David was anointed king long before he took the throne. Throughout scripture, we observe this pattern of divine timing that seldom aligns with human impatience.

Learning to trust in the waiting is perhaps the greatest test of faith. It's easy to believe God has a plan when things are moving quickly, doors are opening, and progress is visible. It's much harder to maintain that conviction when nothing seems to happen or when circumstances seem to go against our hopes.

But it's precisely during these waiting periods that our faith deepens, our character develops, and our capacity to receive what God is preparing expands. The pause isn't punishment or divine negligence — it's preparation.

Your Divine Plan Practices

These practices are designed to help you trust God's prosperous plans for your life, even when the way isn't clear. They will support you in recognizing divine guidance from your past, physically feeling what it's like to embrace God's future for you, and honestly assessing where God's timing may differ from your own expectations. Remember, your current circumstances—no matter how hard or confusing—are not the end of your story but just part of God's larger narrative of hope and purpose for your life.

1. Journal Prompt

Reflect on your life and recall times when God's plans turned out to be better than yours. Maybe it was hard to see His plan at the moment. How did you learn to trust Him while you waited? How does it feel to know that God has plans to prosper you, even when the way forward is uncertain?

2. Embodiment Exercise: Trusting God's Plans

Sit or stand comfortably, close your eyes, and take a few deep breaths. Focus on your breath and bring your awareness to the present moment.

Imagine yourself in the future, having embraced the plans that God has for you. What does your life look like? How do you feel knowing you're right where God wants you to be?

As you breathe deeply, say: "I trust in God's perfect plan for my life. I believe He is guiding me toward a future filled with hope and prosperity."

Open your eyes and stretch your arms, symbolizing your readiness to embrace the future God has planned for you. Feel the peace that comes from knowing His plans are good.

Reflect on how it feels to actively trust in God's plans for your life, especially when the path is unclear.

The promise God made to the exiles through Jeremiah wasn't that they would immediately return home or that their suffering would end right away. It was that their current circumstances—no matter how painful or confusing—weren't the final chapter of their story. God had a future for them that went beyond what they could see or imagine from their limited perspective.

This same promise extends to us today. Our periods of exile, our seasons of uncertainty, our moments of transition—none of these define our final destination. They are simply chapters in a larger story being written by the Author of life itself.

When we accept this truth, we can face even the most uncertain paths with confidence. Not because we know exactly what's ahead, but because we trust the one who guides the future. Not because we never face setbacks or confusion, but because we believe these are temporary states in an eternal journey.

Will you trust in God's plans to prosper you today, even when the road ahead seems unclear?

Chapter 18
Seek First His Kingdom

"But seek first his kingdom and his righteousness, and all these things will be given to you as well." –Matthew 6:33

I was sitting at my desk surrounded by self-help books, with my open browser tabs filled with podcasts and articles, searching for answers to questions my heart was asking, and that's when I remembered this verse. I was seeking for answers outside of God for questions that I should have gone to him with.

Do you seek God first? I haven't always done so, and I still sometimes look for answers by reading books, listening to podcasts, and talking with others, even though I know those aren't the best options. When I've exhausted other sources, I remember that God, the infinite source of all, the creator of everything, the limitless and abundant Father of us all, is the ultimate source.

"Seek me first, the kingdom of God." That's my reminder to stay aligned with God, do His work, and serve, teach, coach, and love people unconditionally, seeing their divinity within and helping them facilitate their healing.

The Radical Invitation

Jesus spoke these words during the Sermon on the Mount. The people Jesus was teaching probably struggled with basic needs like food, clothing, and shelter. Though they weren't wealthy, they cared for their families and themselves. Jesus reminds them to seek God first, and then their basic needs will be provided for.

In this part of Scripture, Jesus explains how this new kingdom functions. He makes a clear comparison between life in the Kingdom of God and the life they were living in Matthew 6:25–32, where He states:

"Therefore, I tell you, do not worry about your life, what you will eat or drink, or about your body, what you will wear. Is not life more than food and the body more than clothes? Look at the birds of the air; they do not sow, reap, or store away in barns, and yet your heavenly Father feeds them. Are you not much more valuable than they? Can any one of you, by worrying, add a single hour to your life? And why do you worry about clothes? See how the flowers of the field grow. They do not labor or spin. Yet I tell you that not even Solomon, in all his splendor, was dressed like one of these. If that is how God clothes the grass of the field, which is here today and tomorrow is thrown into the fire, will he not much more clothe you—you of little faith? So do not worry, saying, 'What shall we eat?' or 'What shall we drink?' or 'What shall we wear?' For the pagans run after all these things, and your heavenly Father knows that you need them."

"Seek first" invites us into a new reality: the realm of the Kingdom of God. It's an exchange. Instead of living based on what we accomplish ourselves, Jesus calls us into a life where provision comes from who we are—as children of God, not from what we do.

Imagine hearing this for the first time: the God of the universe offers to provide everything you need, not only spiritually but also your tangible, physical needs, if you seek His kingdom first. In other words, provision flows from His kingdom because you are His child and He loves you, not based on how you perform or what you achieve.

What "Seek First" Really Means

What does "seek first the kingdom" mean? It means that we turn to God and His kingdom first for everything we need, including our purpose in life, daily needs, creative inspiration, business ideas, family relationships, and all other parts of our lives. As we keep God and our relationship with Him at the center of everything, "all these things will be added unto you."

But seeking Him first doesn't mean just adding God to our list of priorities; it means making Him the central focus around which all other priorities revolve. It involves evaluating every decision, opportunity, and relationship through the lens of divine alignment.

"Seek first the kingdom" means understanding and embracing your unique design within God's kingdom. The special gifts and talents that God has given are meant to enhance your life and be used by Him to unleash the transformative power of His kingdom on earth. As you do this, God is faithful to provide vision, resources, opportunities, and authority to fulfill the purpose He has created for you. Walking in your God-given assignment ensures His favor and provision in your life.

I spent years of my life not putting God first, but instead chasing external validation and achievements. It was my preferred drug. It was the energy that powered each day. Not because it was satisfying, but because I convinced myself it was easier than living in faith. I told myself it was simpler to try to control circumstances on my own than to hand them over to God, who created me and the entire universe. It sounds crazy as I write these words. Everything changed for me when I made God the focus of my life.

The Paradox of Divine Provision

There's a beautiful paradox in this teaching. When we focus less on our needs and more on God's purposes, our needs are met more abundantly than when we focus on them directly. It's counterintuitive to our achievement-oriented culture, but it aligns perfectly with spiritual wisdom.

When we chase after material security, accomplishments, or recognition directly, we often find ourselves on an endless treadmill. There's always more to gain, achieve, or prove. When we align with divine purpose—serving others, creating value, living with integrity, and pursuing justice and compassion—we often discover that our needs are met in unexpected ways.

Consider focusing on breathing rather than trying to control your heartbeat. You can choose to take deep breaths, but you can't force your heart to beat slower. When you concentrate on breathing properly, your heart naturally finds its rhythm. The same principle applies to God's provision. When I fixate on chasing after things—money, status, recognition—I constantly strive and am never satisfied. But when I prioritize serving others and following God's purpose, the things I need come in ways I couldn't have planned. It's counterintuitive, but it works. Give first, then receive.

Living from Divine Identity

Journal Entry, January 18, 2024

Good morning! Lord, I love you so much! I feel so good. I am so excited to be as big as you created me to be! So big that my energy is so magnetizing that what you have in store for me comes to me so easily!

I plan to apply to at least one TEDx stage, and they will say "yes." One step at a time. It's already happened; it's been inside me for so long. I am already there, in my burgundy dress, feeling confident and fully embodied. Helping people live the full width of their lives means encouraging them to bring more of themselves into their everyday experiences. Proactively living and being the main character in their own stories.

We're still in the garden, just confused, playing out these parts. What if all of that is true? There is no time, and there is no separation from God. Are we still asleep? But Jesus said the veil is torn. Does that mean we must listen to "If you have eyes, see. If you have ears, hear."? We are capable of both if we seek God first. I can feel the connection in worship, prayer, the stillness of meditation, in nature, and in the activation of breath.

Lord, work through me. Speak to me, speak through me, love through me— may it be less of me and more of You!

I am living each day doing what I need to do. God is taking care of the rest. He has, is, and will support me fully. His ways are not our ways—they are better if we get out of His way.

I believe that God has fully equipped me with everything I need to fulfill my part in His timing. All will be revealed as it should be.

It's easy to fall into the trap of trying to prove to others that I'm successful. That never made me feel good or at peace with my life. Now, I have more freedom, abundance, joy, and purpose. I want to enjoy all that I have instead of worrying about it. Thank you, God! Show me how to serve everyone I meet today.

Those who faithfully manage the little they have will be promoted and trusted with greater responsibilities. However, those who cheat with what they have will not be seen as trustworthy enough to receive more.

So, I always show up big and faithful today.

This journal entry highlights the freedom that comes from prioritizing the kingdom first, not freedom from responsibility or action, but freedom from the anxiety, comparison, and striving that often accompany our pursuits. When we align with divine purpose, we can dream big dreams without tying our worth to their fulfillment. We can take bold action without being paralyzed by fear of failure. We can celebrate others' success without feeling threatened or diminished.

Pathways to Kingdom-First Living

Seeking the kingdom first isn't a one-time decision; it's a daily choice. Here are some practical ways to nurture this divine priority.

1. Begin Each Day in Divine Connection

Start your morning by connecting with God before engaging with the world. Whether through prayer, meditation, scripture, or silent contemplation, build your relationship with the divine as the foundation for everything else.

Many of us reach for our phones first thing in the morning, instantly immersing ourselves in information, demands, and the priorities of others. Instead, focus on spiritual connection first. Let your first thoughts be directed toward God, rather than tasks, news, or social media.

2. Filter Decisions Through Kingdom Values

When faced with choices, whether big or small, ask yourself: "What aligns most closely with God's kingdom values of love, truth, justice, mercy, and wholeness?" Let these values guide your decisions, rather than prioritizing convenience, popularity, or personal gain.

This doesn't mean every decision turns into a major spiritual crisis. Instead, it's about developing spiritual reflexes that automatically align with the divine.

3. Practice Present-Moment Awareness

The kingdom of God isn't just a future hope — it's a present reality we can fully participate in right now. Develop awareness of God's presence in everyday moments, recognizing the sacred in the ordinary.

When we are fully present, we are more likely to notice divine guidance, recognize opportunities to serve, and experience gratitude for provisions already received. Presence is the soil in which kingdom-first living grows.

4. Redefine Success Through Kingdom Metrics

Our culture measures success through achievement, acquisition, and approval. Kingdom metrics emphasize impact over income, service over status, character over credentials, and relationships over recognition.

This doesn't mean that material prosperity is wrong; it means that it's a potential byproduct rather than the main goal. When we measure success by kingdom impact, we are freed from the endless treadmill of cultural expectations.

5. Surrender Outcomes While Remaining Faithful to Process

Seeking first the kingdom means fulfilling your role without trying to control the results. Plant and water the seeds, but trust God for the growth. Take inspired action, but let go of attachment to specific outcomes or timing.

This balance of faithful action and surrendering outcomes opens the way for divine provision to appear in unexpected ways. We do our part; God does what only God can do.

Your Kingdom-First Practices

Experience the freedom that comes from putting God's kingdom first. These practices will help you recognize where you might be looking for answers outside of God, feel what it's like to focus on divine purposes rather than personal needs, and honestly evaluate your current priorities in key areas of life. Jesus didn't add another burden to your busy life; He offered a complete reset that centers your relationship with God, allowing everything else to fall into its proper place.

1. Journal Prompt

Do you seek God first or turn to other sources for answers? Journal on any feelings of scarcity or lack regarding material needs. How can you shift your focus to God's purposes and trust that He will provide for you?

2. Embodiment Exercise: Centering on God's Kingdom

Sit or stand comfortably, close your eyes, and take a few deep breaths to center yourself.

Imagine a world where God's love, peace, and justice fill every part of your life. See yourself living in harmony with His plans and feeling safe and at peace with His provision.

As you take a deep breath, say: "I seek first Your kingdom, Lord. I trust that You will provide for all my needs."

Release any anxieties or worries you've been carrying about material needs, finances, or personal success. Visualize these burdens lifting from your shoulders as you focus on God's promises.

Take a few moments to sit quietly and reflect on what it feels like to surrender your worries to God and focus on His kingdom. Write down any insights or thoughts that come to mind.

The invitation to "seek first the kingdom" isn't a burden—it's a liberation. It frees us from the exhausting effort of trying to secure our own provision, prove our own worth, or determine our own purpose. It releases us into the flow of divine abundance that comes not from striving but from being in alignment.

When we fully understand this teaching, we see that Jesus wasn't just adding another demand to our busy lives. Instead, He was offering a new way of living that focuses on our relationship with God and lets everything else revolve around that divine connection.

The promise remains just as true today as when Jesus first spoke it: seek first the kingdom, and everything else you need will be provided. Not because you've earned it through spiritual effort, but because you are a beloved child of the One who owns everything and takes pleasure in providing for you.

Will you make seeking first the kingdom your priority today?

Chapter 19

The Light for Your Path

"Your word is a lamp to my feet and a light to my path."
–Psalm 119:105

I've always wanted to see the entire staircase before taking the first step. Whenever I consider a major life change—such as switching careers, moving to a new city, or starting a creative project—I find myself obsessing over having every detail planned out before I begin. I seek certainty. I crave guarantees. I need to know exactly how things will unfold.

Maybe you can relate. One of my biggest challenges, and what I often see with my clients, is the desire to know all the steps before starting. For some reason, we focus on the "how" before we get clear on the "what or why." We want to know how it will turn out before we even begin.

This struggle is not new. These words come from Psalm 119, the longest Psalm in the Bible. It is attributed to King David and reminds us that God's Word is the light and guide for our journey and path. King David loved God deeply, and God loved him in return. He meditated on God's Word and trusted that it would provide the illumination he needed.

Enough Light for Today

What I've learned on my journey is that although God may provide enough light for today, we need to take aligned action to see more of the path illuminated. Our actions create momentum and synchronicities. When I've made big leaps in my life, it wasn't because I had all the steps figured out. I pray daily to hear from God and see what I need for the day. Light my path today. Illuminate my path just a few steps, so I don't get off track.

When I realized that, I felt at ease. I understood I didn't need to see the entire path or journey. I am given God's Word and scripture verses as a lamp when I need them. This book shows how often I rely on the Word of God to give me what I need. The inspiration, courage, conviction, redirection, encouragement, peace, grace, and love are provided.

Think about how a lamp worked in ancient times. It didn't light up the whole path ahead; it only cast enough light for a few steps. In the darkness, that was enough to move forward safely. I believe divine guidance often works similarly—not revealing the entire journey at once, but providing just enough clarity for the next step.

This doesn't mean we move forward blindly or aimlessly. It means we trust that with each guided step, the light will accompany us, revealing what was once hidden. The path reveals itself as we walk it.

The Paradox of Illumination

There's a beautiful paradox in this scripture: the lamp doesn't eliminate all darkness; it transforms how we relate to it. The darkness still exists beyond the circle of light, but it no longer keeps us trapped or blocks our progress. We can move forward confidently within the lit space, knowing we have what we need for now.

When I heard during my meditation that I should write this book, I wasn't sure if I could or even if I wanted to. I worried because I didn't feel qualified. I listened to the nudge to revisit my morning writings and see how often I referenced Scripture when facing a challenge or experience. I was surprised to find it was more often than I remembered.

This particular verse is meaningful to me because I struggle with patience. It is not my natural state. Patience may be the fruit of the Spirit I find most difficult. Of course, I want to see the whole staircase or the entire journey, which is why my lesson requires faith. I've worked on this because I've been repeatedly shown that God does light my path; He lights it for what I need today. And that is enough.

The lamp doesn't replace the need for faith; instead, it complements it. The light guides us where to step, while faith gives us the courage to move forward. One without the other leaves us either stuck or stumbling in darkness.

Taking the Illuminated Step

Journal Entry, July 28, 2022

I always tell my clients to follow the energy, and that energy guides me straight to launching my podcast. I am so excited, I can't contain my enthusiasm. I love interviewing people I know and those I don't, especially those living extraordinary lives. I want to hear how they achieved it—how they overcame fears, learned to dream again, and the importance of managing their energy. How do they take care of themselves? I love the idea of recording myself talking to people and allowing their light to shine through.

Watching the news is disappointing. It seems like it's curated to make us feel bad. I want my show to inspire others. I'm manifesting the most amazing guests. Please show me who else should join the show. Who is living their best life? Who is doing something really cool?

I trust and believe in God to light my path, sometimes taking one step at a time—opening doors, closing doors, redirecting, supporting, and uplifting me. The staircase is there; I can only see one or two steps ahead. But I'm more comfortable not seeing the entire staircase because, guess what? Predicting it only limits it. God's plans are bigger, brighter, and more exciting than anything else.

I am so grateful for my life, my family, our health, our beautiful home, fresh water, healthy food, my friends, the ability to do what I love, to help others, the people you've brought into my life, the open doors and closed doors. Thank you for showing me the way. I love and trust you!

Reading this journal entry, I realized something important: when we try to predict everything, we limit ourselves. It's like we're telling God, "I can only go as far as I can see right now." But God's plans are much bigger than what we can imagine. When I stopped demanding to see the whole staircase and just took the step in front of me, amazing things started to happen. Doors opened that I never knew existed. People showed up that I couldn't have planned to meet. Opportunities appeared that weren't even on my radar. By taking that first step with just enough light to see, I walked into possibilities far beyond what I could have imagined if I'd insisted on seeing everything first.

Reflecting on my life, I realize there were times when I was stuck in my spiritual growth. It wasn't that God had stopped; I was stuck because I wasn't using the guidance and light I was given to take the next step. Now, I do my best to take that next step whenever it presents itself. I might stumble or do it scared, but I know it's my turn to move forward.

The Multiple Dimensions of Illumination

Scripture, as the lamp to my feet and the light to my path, provides multiple forms of guidance:

Visibility in Darkness

Think about how a lamp works in the dark. It doesn't entirely remove the darkness, but it changes how we see it. God's Word is similar during tough times—when we're grieving, confused, disappointed, or facing big changes. Scripture doesn't erase these hard experiences, but it helps us see them differently and guides us through them.

When I face tough decisions or feel lost, diving into Scripture reminds me that I am not the first to walk this path. Others have been here before me and found their way forward. Their stories serve as my guides. Reading about how David dealt with betrayal or how Ruth managed a total life change provides me with a perspective I can't find when I am stuck in my own head with a limited view.

Direction When Lost

Light doesn't just shine; it guides. When I feel lost or unsure about my next step, God's Word becomes my compass. It directs me toward what matters most, even when I can't see clearly what's right in front of me.

Scripture teaches me to choose love over fear, to give rather than take, to embrace courage over comfort, and to prioritize connection instead of isolation. These core truths guide me even in situations I've never faced before. They help me make complex decisions by focusing on what truly matters.

Safety Among Hazards

A lamp not only shows the way but also reveals dangers—the stones that might trip us and the drops we need to avoid. God's Word does the same in our lives. It warns us about choices and patterns that could harm us or lead us astray.

These warnings aren't meant to scare us—they're meant to guide us toward better choices. They help us recognize patterns that might seem appealing in the moment but lead to long-term difficulty or disconnection from our deepest values. I've learned that these spiritual guardrails aren't limitations—they're protection for my freedom and joy.

Confirmation of Progress

Light not only reveals what's ahead; it also shows us where we've been. When I read Scripture regularly, I notice changes in myself that I might otherwise miss. I see growth taking place. I recognize patterns shifting. I observe transformation happening in my heart and mind.

This is why I love journaling so much. When I look back at entries from months or years ago, I can see the journey I've been on. I notice the struggles that once seemed overwhelming, but God helped me through them. I recognize the wisdom I've gained along the way. I find evidence of God's faithfulness that I might have otherwise forgotten if I hadn't written it down.

The more I spend time with God's Word, the more I see it illuminate every part of my life—including my mind, experiences, relationships, choices, and heart. It's not just about memorizing verses; it's about letting God's truth shine from the inside out.

Practical Ways to Light Your Path

If you truly believe that God's Word is a lamp for your feet, how do you incorporate it into your daily routine? Here are some ways to help you stay within that circle of light.

1. Daily Time in the Word

Reading Scripture regularly helps you develop a reserve of wisdom to turn to during difficult times. It's like gaining access to God's perspective exactly when it's needed. Just a few minutes of reading each day can help you become more familiar with God's voice and point of view.

You just need to show up consistently in the Word. Over time, certain verses will become ingrained and accessible for you to draw upon in different situations. They'll become part of who you are, woven into your spiritual DNA.

2. Sitting With the Word

When you take time to sit with a verse or passage—whether to ponder it, journal about it, or meditate on it—it sinks more deeply into your heart. Ask yourself, "What does this mean for my life right now? How does this connect to what I'm going through?" Don't be afraid to sit with the words. Let the Holy Spirit guide you.

This quiet reflection transforms Scripture from just intellectual knowledge into wisdom you apply in your daily choices. It's the difference between knowing about light and actually walking in it.

3. Sharing Insights with Others

Discussing Scripture with friends, small groups, or online helps you see new perspectives. Others notice things you overlook or applications you hadn't thought of. Their insights fill your blind spots.

We're not meant to figure everything out on our own. Throughout history, people have come together to discuss sacred texts because they value each other's wisdom. When you share thoughts about God's Word with others, your understanding deepens and becomes more complete.

4. Taking Action Opens New Doors

Here's what matters most: more light often appears when you act on what you already know. Moving forward with the light you have today makes tomorrow's path clearer. If you wait until everything is perfectly clear before acting, you might actually delay the guidance you're seeking.

This doesn't mean making impulsive decisions. It means faithfully responding to what God has already shown you, trusting that He'll reveal the next step when you need it. Each step of obedience invites more understanding.

Your Path of Light Practices

These practices will help you recognize the sources of divine light you rely on, experience what it's like to walk with just enough light for each step, and evaluate which areas of your life currently have sufficient light and which need more. God isn't asking you to see the entire staircase; He's inviting you to take the step that's illuminated right in front of you, trusting that more light will come as you move forward.

1. Journal Prompt

What has been your experience with reading Scripture or other spiritual texts? What sources of inspiration do you rely on when you need guidance? What has God been illuminating for you recently that shows you your next step?

2. Embodiment Exercise: Walking in the Light

Rise to your feet and close your eyes. Take a deep breath to ground yourself.

Imagine walking along a dark trail. Then, picture being given a lamp that lights up the ground right in front of you, showing you where to step next. With each step, the light moves forward as well, revealing the next part of the trail.

As you take deep breaths, say to yourself: "Your Word is a lamp to my feet and a light to my path. I trust that You will guide me."

Visualize each step you take as guided by God's Word, giving you clarity and confidence.

Pause for a moment and notice how it feels to walk in God's light. Write down any thoughts or feelings that come up during this exercise.

The promise in Psalm 119:105 isn't that you'll never face darkness or uncertainty. It's that even in those dark times, you have enough light to guide your path. You might not see the final destination—probably won't—but you can take the next faithful step.

Maybe the greatest act of faith isn't waiting until everything is crystal clear before taking action. Maybe it's trusting that as you take each illuminated step, the light will move with you, revealing things you couldn't see before. The path appears as you walk it.

Will you trust the light you have today and take your next step?

Chapter 20

There Are Giants in the Land— But So Is God

"Do not fear the unknown, for God is already there. He goes before you, preparing the way and guiding you with His light."
–Deuteronomy 31:8

I'm going through another season of uncertainty right now. The world feels very chaotic, and so does my inner dialogue. The voices in my head are loud again, making it hard to sleep, and I fluctuate between being honest with myself about my struggles and writing affirmations and prayers to hide my doubts. Then I feel ashamed of my doubts, disbelief, and wavering faith. It's a cycle I've experienced many times throughout my life.

These words were originally spoken by Moses to the Israelites just before he passed leadership to Joshua. Moses had led his people for decades by this point. He remained faithful to God, but he and the Israelites wandered in the desert for forty years after fleeing Egypt. They were anxious, tired, and God had not yet led them into the Promised Land. However, Moses reassures the Israelites that, although there will be challenges, uncertainties, and enemies, God will not abandon them. God goes before them, prepares the way, and guides them with His light.

When Giants Loom Large

God sent twelve Israelites into the Promised Land, including Joshua and Caleb, to report what they saw. When they returned, ten were overwhelmed by the sight: giants, fortresses, and what seemed like insurmountable obstacles.

"We seemed like grasshoppers in our own eyes, and we looked the same to them" (Numbers 13:33).

The ten men spread fear, doubt, and disbelief to the others in the group.

Only Joshua and Caleb saw something different. Yes, there were giants. But God's promise to them was just as big.

Caleb calmed the people and said, "We should go up and take possession of the land, for we can certainly do it." (Numbers 13:30)

He wasn't ignoring the size of the giants in the Promise Land. He was trusting in the size of God's faithfulness.

And yet, the others chose fear over faith. They preferred safety instead of surrender. Because they lacked faith in God's promise, they wandered in the wilderness for forty years until the unbelieving generation passed away.

Only Joshua and Caleb entered the Promised Land from the original group. Only the faithful saw the promise fulfilled.

Modern-Day Giants

Today, our giants look different. They carry names like fear, shame, scarcity, failure, and rejection. They stand tall, shout lies, and like the Israelites, we're tempted to retreat and forget who goes before us.

These struggles are universal and have been part of the human experience since the beginning of time. As an entrepreneur, I am aware of my dependence on God every day. I rely on God's will, blessings, and provision for the money coming into my business. I don't receive a paycheck every two weeks from a company; it comes from clients who want to work with me.

It's easy to convince myself that it's my effort, but it's not. It's God's provision and blessing. It has always been that way, even before I started my business.

When we face uncertainty—whether in business, relationships, health, or any other area—we often focus on the size of our giants instead of the size of our God. We compare obstacles to our own strength rather than divine power. We forget that the same God who parted seas, brought down walls, and transformed lives still goes before us today.

Divine Preparation in Uncertain Seasons

As I read this verse, I just journaled about what I'm feeling right now:

Journal Entry, March 14, 2025

Lord, show me Your will for my life. I often find myself pushing, striving, and seeking action, yet I hear You telling me to slow down, rest, pause, listen quietly, and remain in the spaciousness of the unknown. Like a child having a meltdown, I feel the tears dry, my breath slows, my body softens, and the resistance lifts. I return to You, the only true source of peace and stillness, and I feel held and reminded that You love me, that Your plans are greater than mine, and that You are preparing me for greatness.

"Not yet," I hear you say. "Stay here a little while. Integrate. Give yourself space to breathe, to grow, to prepare. Let me prepare you and the way. I know where I am taking you. I know the timing, my will, my anointing, my pace, and my purpose for you.

"Don't try to be anyone else but who I created you to be. Get your systems in place; that's what you need to do now. I am preparing you for more. It will pay off. Invest now. It will pay off. Learn more. Test and learn. I'll guide you. I am guiding you. There are no mistakes.

"Growth happens even when you don't see it. My ways are not your ways. Relax, rest, breathe deeply, and release resistance. Let go of the need to know and see everything. Trust me. Believe in my promises. I am God.

"What do you need right now?"

I reply, "Health for my family, safety, and security. I know this is what I need to feel safe. I seek confirmation that I'm on the right track, doing Your will, and that this business You and I built aligns with Your will. I realize I see the money and clients coming in as validation from You that I'm doing the right things, that I'm serving, and that I'm aligned with You. Is that right? Am I viewing this correctly? How will I know the difference?"

Walking By Faith, Not By Sight

Looking at this journal entry, I realize something important about these uncertain times in our lives. They're not just periods when we're stuck waiting—they're sacred moments when God is preparing us. There is a sacred space between rest and readying. When I feel impatient or frustrated by a lack of movement, God might be using that very space to prepare me for what's coming next.

I'm learning that sometimes true faith isn't about rushing but about being still. Not because I'm scared, but because I'm listening. Not because I'm giving up, but because I'm handing over control to God, who sees everything I can't see yet.

It happens every time I hit a low point. Somehow, God leads me to exactly the verse I need to read. This time wasn't different. I needed these words: "Do not fear the unknown, for God is already there. He goes before you, preparing the way and guiding you with His light."

These words remind me that I don't need to fear what I cannot see or predict. My God—who created everything and knows everything—is already in my tomorrow. He has been there. He's not surprised by my fears or when I doubt. He's already preparing my path and lighting my way, just as He has always done.

I want to be more like Joshua and Caleb. Not pretending the giants aren't real—they definitely are—but trusting deep down that God is more real than any obstacle I face.

I want my faith to go beyond what my eyes can see. I desire to trust even when I don't feel like it. I want to receive God's blessings, not because I've earned them, but because I believe they're already mine.

My promised land awaits me. It's not just a physical place I want to reach; it's a way of life. It's choosing faith over fear, following God's guidance instead of trying to control everything, and trusting in what God has promised—even when it seems impossible from my perspective.

I pray that I will be found faithful, one of the few who sees the giants and still moves forward.

Practical Ways to Face Your Giants

How can we practically live out the faith of Joshua and Caleb in a world full of giants? Here are some strategies to help you remain steadfast when faced with uncertainty.

1. Call Out Your Giants By Name

The Israelite spies didn't just say, "It's scary." They specifically described what they saw. There's power in naming exactly what scares you. Not to give it more power, but to bring it into the light where you can measure it against God's promises.

Take a moment to write down the specific fears or obstacles that seem overwhelming right now. I've noticed that once I put them on paper, they often begin to lose their hold on me.

2. Remember What God Has Already Done

It's crazy how the Israelites witnessed the Red Sea part, ate manna from heaven, and drank water from rocks—yet still doubted God when facing the next challenge. I catch myself doing the same thing. We forget that we are witnessing miracles every day.

Begin recording the times God has helped you. These stories serve as proof when doubt creeps in, and challenges feel overwhelming.

3. Choose Who You Listen To

Ten spies spread fear while only two showed faith, and the people listened to the majority with devastating results. Who we surround ourselves with matters more than we realize.

Find people who see opportunities where others only see obstacles. These faith-filled voices can help you view things from God's perspective when fear begins to cloud your judgment.

4. Take One Brave Step

Caleb didn't just talk about faith; he was ready to act on it. "We should go up and take possession of the land, for we can certainly do it." God doesn't just want us to believe the right things; He wants those beliefs to motivate us.

What's one small, brave step you can take today toward what God has promised? It doesn't have to be the whole journey—just the next faithful step.

5. Focus on God, Not the Giants

The Israelites couldn't stop staring at the giants and completely lost sight of the God who had promised them the land.

When facing uncertainty, intentionally shift your focus from the size of your problems to the size of your God. It's not about pretending challenges aren't real but seeing them from a higher perspective.

Your Giant-Facing Practices

Face your giants with faith, not fear. Identify the specific unknowns that cause anxiety in your life. Physically feel what it's like to move forward, confident that God has gone ahead of you. Evaluate how your challenges compare to His power, not just your own strength. Remember, this isn't about pretending your giants aren't real—it's about knowing that wherever your giants are, God is already there, too.

1. Journal Prompt

What "unknowns" in your life are causing you fear right now? How can you trust God to guide you through them? Write about how you can take the next step forward, even if you can't see the whole path.

2. Embodiment Exercise: Walking with Confidence

Stand with your feet shoulder-width apart. Close your eyes and take a deep breath.

Imagine standing at the start of a dark path. Ahead, there is a light. As you walk toward it, the path becomes clearer with every step.

As you move forward, tell yourself: "God goes before me. I am not alone. He prepares the way." Feel how it shifts your body to realize God has already gone ahead of you.

Pause and reflect on the unknowns in your life. How does it feel to know that God has already been there? How can you move forward with more confidence?

The story of the twelve Israelites teaches us that what we focus on grows larger. Ten saw only giants, while two saw the God who was greater than any obstacle. The difference wasn't what they saw, but how they saw it.

Today, you face a similar choice. Yes, there are giants in your land—real challenges, genuine fears, and valid concerns. This isn't about pretending they're not there. It's about remembering that wherever giants appear, God is right there too.

He goes before you into every unknown. He prepares the way when the path seems impossible. He brings light when darkness surrounds you. Not because the journey will be easy, but because you never walk it alone.

Will you be among those who see the giants, or among those who see God?

Chapter 21

Exceeding Abundance

"Now to Him who is able to do exceedingly abundantly beyond all that we ask or imagine, according to the power that works in us."
–Ephesians 3:20

Our God is LIMITLESS. His intentions are generous, and His power already lives within us. He calls us to believe confidently, ask courageously, and live with expectation. Because the limitations we see as real are false beliefs that only exist in our minds. Every time I struggle or have anxious thoughts, it's because I am focused on my limited abilities instead of the limitless nature of God.

This verse isn't about what we can do. It's about God's power. It offers a foundation we can depend on: God can. Period. No matter what challenge we face or how impossible things appear, God is able. These words call us to trust Him completely, reminding us that God isn't limited by our circumstances, our bank accounts, or our past setbacks.

Beyond Our Imagination

When Paul writes about God doing "exceedingly abundantly beyond all that we ask or imagine..." he highlights the overflowing nature of God's blessings and plans. Notice how he doesn't just say "more than," but intentionally stacks these powerful words: *exceedingly, abundantly, beyond.* Paul uses language that truly goes above and beyond what we can even describe.

This reminds me that God dreams bigger for us than we do for ourselves. The things I pray for, hope for, and dare to imagine—God is already thinking beyond that. My biggest vision is just the beginning of what God has planned.

I've had times when I thought I was praying boldly, only to realize later that God had something much greater planned. It's like asking for a glass of water and receiving an ocean.

The Power Within

When Paul says, "According to the power that works in us..." he's telling us that this divine power operates within us. It's not distant or abstract. It's the Holy Spirit's power in us, aligning our hearts with limitless possibilities.

We are not passive recipients; we are active participants. When we walk in faith, align with God's will, and act in obedience, we activate the power already within us.

I've observed this pattern many times in my life. When I try to do things on my own, they might turn out okay or even good, but I usually end up exhausted. However, when I first align with God, invite His guidance, strength, and help, and let God work through me and on my behalf, that's when true miracles happen. That's when things turn out even better than I ever imagined.

Paul's Perspective from Prison

Paul wrote this passage while he was in prison. Think about that for a moment. He's sitting in a jail cell, writing to the Ephesians about God's overwhelming love and generosity. From behind bars, he's reminding them of God's unwavering commitment to provide "exceedingly abundantly" beyond what we can imagine.

Can you grasp what this means for us? God isn't interested in giving us just enough to get by. He's the God of overflow, abundance, and limitless possibilities. His love flows out like a well that never runs dry. When we allow Him to work through us, both our lives and those around us are transformed. We become vessels carrying His extraordinary power and love into an ordinary world.

Breaking Free from Hustle Culture

I've spent much of my life rushing from one thing to another. I was immersed in hustle culture from a very young age. I watched my parents and grandparents work tirelessly as they built a new life here in the United States, and I saw their hard work pay off in many ways. I also saw it benefit me in school and in my career. I never hesitated to work beyond the point where my mind and body told me it was enough.

The warning signs that I was taking on too much showed up in 2011. I was working full-time, raising two middle school girls, managing a team at work, and enrolled in a full-time MBA program. I had two back-to-back surgeries in October and November 2011, one on my breast and the other on my ovary. Fortunately, they weren't life-threatening, but I spent weeks waiting for results and feeling uncertain.

There's nothing quite like a health scare to wake you up. That's how it felt for me. That moment prompted me to start making changes and question whether I was truly living the life God had planned for me. I also asked Him for help. I began taking a day of rest.

Resting gave me time to reflect, connect with God, and access the inner wisdom of my soul. I began to ask myself important questions about what I truly want, why I am here, and if I would die with regret if something were to happen to me.

Remembering Who We Are

Journal Entry, December 18, 2018

I am not here to accomplish, achieve, or earn. Each of us is here on this planet to remember who we are and whose we are. We are eternal souls, without birth or death. We are divinely created by You, our heavenly creator, and we will always return to the source, which is God. Our job is to remember WHO we are, grow to discover our unique, special gifts, and fulfill our purpose. We each have our own race to run, and we are uniquely equipped to do what we are called to do. God Himself equips us to do what HE called us to do. And, the plans He has for us are much bigger and better than we can ever imagine.

I am preparing for the amazing destiny that You have planned for me. I know that You fully support me as I help a limitless number of people globally create transformational change. I believe, down to my cellular level, that You have BIG plans for my life to help others. You have equipped me with everything I need; therefore, I need not worry. And everything I have learned, I will share with others. We are creating lanterns of light around the world.

Looking back, I realize that 2011 was when everything began to change in my life. I started reading Scripture again. I dedicated time every day to pray and meditate. The more I practiced, the more I believed that something bigger and better was possible for my life. I allowed myself to believe that God's power was within me and that I could tap into it to do even more than I thought or imagined.

Expanding Our Vision

This verse is so powerful because it reminds us that we don't need to have all the answers. Our vision isn't as big as God's vision for us. Instead of being afraid that we want too much, or that what we're imagining is too big, or that we can't possibly figure out how to make it happen, we don't need to do the heavy lifting. God does that for us. We just need to connect with that energy.

I've found that most of us don't dream big enough.

We limit ourselves based on:

What We've Seen Before

We often think of the future as just slightly better versions of our pasts. But God isn't limited by what has been; He's skilled at creating what has never existed.

What We Think We Deserve

Many of us unconsciously lower our expectations based on what we think we deserve. But God's abundance comes from His nature, not our worthiness.

What We Think Is Possible

Our minds naturally estimate probabilities based on visible resources and known pathways. However, God works with unseen resources and opens new pathways.

What Others Tell Us to Expect

Sometimes, we accept others' limited expectations for our lives. However, God has His own plans for us that often surpass what humans expect.

When we realize that God's ability to provide exceeds what we can imagine, something changes. We stop trying to figure everything out and instead concentrate on where God is already at work. We become less focused on forcing things and more attentive to joining in what He's already doing.

From Striving to Receiving

The word "exceedingly" reminds me that God isn't interested in just meeting the minimum requirements. When God provides, He does so generously, extravagantly, beyond what was asked for.

This isn't just about material wealth; it's about experiencing peace, purpose, joy, love, healing, wisdom, and making an impact. It's about living with an abundance mindset rather than one of scarcity in every aspect of life.

The shift from striving to receiving doesn't mean becoming passive; it means redirecting our effort from trying to control everything ourselves to being open to what God is already eager to give. It involves investing more energy in listening than in planning and focusing more on alignment than on achievement.

Your Abundant Life Practices

I've developed two exercises to help you experience God's abundant life. These will guide you in identifying areas where you've been relying on your own strength instead of divine power, physically feeling what it's like to expand your imagination beyond self-imposed limits, and assessing specific ways you might position yourself to receive more than you've been asking for. Remember, this isn't about what you can achieve through effort—it's about what God can do through you when you tap into the limitless power He's already placed within you.

1. Journal Prompt

Which areas of your life have you been trying to handle on your own instead of trusting in God's abundant power? How would things change if you believed you could access God's strength? What stops you from expecting this level of abundance?

2. Embodiment Exercise: Expanding Your Imagination

Sit comfortably with your feet flat on the ground and your hands resting on your lap. Close your eyes, breathe deeply a few times, and relax into your body.

Imagine a part of your life where you seek God's abundance. Visualize what you would ask for, then allow yourself to imagine something even greater—something beyond your wildest dreams.

As you hold that vision, quietly say to yourself: "God's power to do exceedingly abundantly more is within me." Feel your heart expand as your dreams and expectations grow.

Open your eyes and think about what it was like to imagine beyond your usual limits. How can you begin to walk in faith, knowing that God's abundance is greater than you ever thought possible?

Ephesians 3:20 invites us into a life that goes beyond what we can imagine on our own. Not because we've earned it or can accomplish it through effort, but because this is who God is—extravagantly generous by nature.

As you close this chapter, I encourage you to ask for bigger things, dream without limits, and trust that God will show up in remarkable ways. Not out of entitlement but from deep trust in the One who can do infinitely more than you could ever ask for.

You might feel stuck right now because of your circumstances, limited resources, or drained energy. But remember: the God of "exceedingly abundantly beyond" is already at work within you. The real question isn't whether God can do it — it's whether you're positioned to receive what He's already prepared.

Will you open your heart to God's exceeding abundance today?

Section 5

TRANSFORMATION & GROWTH

Chapter 22

Enlarging Your Tent

"Enlarge the place of your tent, stretch your tent curtains wide, do not hold back; lengthen your cords, strengthen your stakes."
–Isaiah 54:2

I still remember the day this verse came to me again. I was sitting in my home office, doing my morning pages and thinking about my business. As I thought about scaling, growing, and expanding in new ways, I felt myself becoming anxious, and my faith wavered. That's when I remembered this verse, looked it up to read it in full, and the words jumped off the page: *Enlarge your tent.* Not "maintain your tent" or "be grateful for your small tent." *Enlarge it.* At that moment, I realized how my own limited thinking had become the ceiling for what God wanted to do through me.

When these words were first spoken, the prophet Isaiah was speaking to the Israelites in exile. They had lost everything and could barely imagine restoration, much less abundance. Yet here was God, telling them to prepare for growth beyond their wildest dreams. He wasn't just promising to meet their needs; He was asking them to make room for overflow.

This verse has challenged me repeatedly to dream bigger dreams. It's a divine invitation to expand our capacity, grow beyond our self-imposed limits, and strengthen ourselves for the abundance God desires. It's not about greed or materialism — it's about making more space for Him in our lives so He can pour His blessings through us to others. When we enlarge our vision and trust in faith, we prepare for something greater than we could achieve on our own.

"Enlarge the place of your tent"

God is calling us to dream bigger and expand our vision of what's possible. This invitation isn't just for one person, it's for anyone seeking a deeper connection with their divine purpose.

I have spent most of my life taking small, steady steps. In school, I followed the rules to get good grades and earn my teachers' approval. In my corporate career, I stuck to the usual path, chasing promotions and raises. I achieved goals, received recognition, and celebrated briefly before moving on to the next level. These small wins of external validation kept me going—until they didn't.

Every morning before going to work, I would stand in front of the mirror, not just putting on makeup but also building my emotional armor. My shoulders would tense, my jaw would tighten, and I could feel myself physically shrinking to meet expectations that weren't meant for my spirit. My colleagues saw a successful executive, but inside, I felt my soul aching.

"Stretch your tent curtains wide"

This is an invitation to embrace new possibilities and unexpected opportunities. It's about saying "yes" when God nudges you toward unfamiliar territory.

When I left my corporate job, it wasn't because I believed I would find success elsewhere. I left because I knew I couldn't stay—my soul was craving alignment. My body was showing signs through chronic fatigue, tension headaches, and a constant feeling of heaviness, indicating I wasn't living in full integrity with my values and purpose.

My initial business goals had a limited vision: make just enough to cover our bills and sustain our lifestyle. Then, after year one, COVID hit. Instead of seeing it as a setback, I did what I know how to do—adapt and keep showing up. Surprisingly, I earned more during the pandemic than I did the year before. My next goal was simply to match my corporate salary and then exceed it.

I was still thinking incrementally, while God was trying to show me exponentially.

"Do not hold back"

God guides us to move past old patterns, limiting beliefs, or stories that block our growth. What brought you here won't take you to where God wants to lead you.

When I re-read Isaiah 54:2 during a difficult time, it scared me. The message was clear: "Do not look back. Only look forward." Enlarge the place of your tent, which means dream bigger; you're expanding, stretching, and growing. God was asking me to let go of my attachment to familiar ways and standards. He was calling me to keep moving forward even when things became uncomfortable or difficult.

I realized that my pattern of incremental thinking was a form of fear—fear that God wouldn't provide, fear that I didn't deserve abundance, fear that I would somehow disappoint others by fully embracing my purpose. These fears were constant worries about finances, despite all evidence that God had always provided, even when I wasn't fully aligned with my calling.

These fears are common and affect people at every stage of life. The young graduate hesitates to pursue their true calling because of student debt. The parent puts their dreams on hold to focus on their children's needs. The mid-career professional resists changing careers even though they feel deeply unsatisfied. The retiree holds back from new ventures, believing their best contributions are behind them. In each case, the message remains the same: "Do not hold back."

"Lengthen your cords, strengthen your stakes"

We need to build the infrastructure to support the growth God has planned for us. It's time to reinforce our foundations—our spiritual practices, mindset, relationships, and skills.

Lengthening and strengthening aren't about trying harder on your own. It's about deepening your connection with the divine so you can receive guidance and strength for the journey ahead. It's about reinforcing your spiritual alignment so that your life flows from your essence rather than your ego.

When I prioritized my morning practice, everything shifted. By investing in my spiritual growth as intentionally as I did in my personal development, my capacity grew without the burnout I used to encounter. I wasn't doing more through willpower; I was achieving more through alignment with divine guidance and flow.

This principle applies whether you're a student preparing for exams, a parent raising children, an entrepreneur developing a business, a teacher shaping young minds, or a retiree discovering a new purpose. The supports that hold your tent are your spiritual practices, community connections, and self-care routines, and they must be strengthened as your vision expands. Growth without reinforcement leads to collapse.

A Glimpse into My Journey

Journal Entry, January 28, 2025

I went to bed feeling worried and anxious. It's the same story. Why haven't I addressed that yet? God has always provided, even when I wasn't living according to my purpose. When I worked at the bank, I pushed myself, put on my armor every day, and made myself small to fit a mold that wasn't meant for me.

I was promoted even then. And now that I have stepped out in faith and am doing what I know God built me for, I worry that He won't provide somehow. That's crazy.

I just had a beautiful meditation and worship. I am crying as I listen to my New Wine playlist. I feel God's presence and the Holy Spirit so strongly. I experience God's unconditional love. Today, as I continue to write my second book, I am reminded to "Enlarge the place of your tent, stretch your tent curtains wide, do not hold back; lengthen your cords, strengthen your stakes. For you will spread out to the right and the left; your descendants will dispossess nations and settle in their desolate cities" (Isaiah 54:2).

This reminds me to dream bigger and expand my faith and beliefs. This verse is all about growth, dreaming bigger, trusting more, grounding myself, and digging deep into my faith; there are no limits to what I can achieve when I am aligned with God. So, I keep returning to serving again and again. How do I show up genuinely and serve with deep faith and trust, knowing that everything is okay? Everything is more than okay.

I'm deeply sorry for my ongoing doubt. I apologize for forgetting. I'm sorry for losing my alignment. I regret allowing doubt to influence me. I'm sorry for stepping away from Your light.

Please forgive me for doubting, forgetting who I am, whose daughter I am, hesitating, hiding, and playing small.

I love You for creating me and for being so good to me.

I share this intimate journal entry because growth isn't linear. Even as I write about enlarging your tent, I still experience moments of contraction and doubt. What has changed is my awareness of these patterns and my tools for returning to trust. The journey of expansion isn't about eliminating fear; it's about not allowing fear to determine your boundaries.

My journal reveals three powerful insights about tent expansion:

1. **Awareness comes before transformation**: Recognizing when you're contracting in fear is the first step toward growing in faith.
2. **Return to spiritual practice**: When doubt arises, meditation and worship help you reconnect with the expansive vision God has for your life.
3. **Self-compassion promotes growth**: Treating yourself with the same kindness that God provides paves the way for true development.

So, I am reminded once again to embrace growth and prosperity and to trust in God's promises. Expansion is already underway. Scale is already happening. We are not meant to stay stagnant where we are. We are made to grow.

I may not be prepared for what God has planned, but I am ready for what I need to do today as part of His plan. That's how growth happens. Sometimes, we don't notice the small steps that occur daily, but that doesn't mean they aren't happening.

Your Tent Expansion Practices

I've created these practices to help you expand your perspective and prepare for the abundance God has planned for you. I hope they will guide you in recognizing areas where God is calling you to grow, physically experience what growth feels like in your body, and identify specific steps you can take to push beyond your current limits. This is about creating more space for God to work through you and pour His blessings out to others.

1. Journal Prompt

As you consider your life as a "tent"—your dreams, relationships, work, and health—where do you feel God is guiding you to expand your perspective and stretch your capacity?

What small steps can you take right now to get ready for the blessings and opportunities He is planning for you?

2. Embodiment Exercise: Expanding Your Capacity

Stand tall with your feet shoulder-width apart. Close your eyes, take a deep breath, and focus on the part of your life where you feel God is calling you to grow.

Gently raise both arms upward, visualizing yourself stretching to make space for all the good things God is preparing. As you lift, take a deep breath and imagine growth and potential.

As you hold the stretch, say: "I am making room for the abundant blessings God is bringing into my life. I am expanding my capacity to receive and grow."

Relax and bring your arms back to your sides. Take a moment to reflect on what it felt like to expand your body physically. How does it feel to envision expanding your life in the same way?

3. Tent Expansion Inventory

- Current size (where you are now)
- Desired expansion (where God might be calling you)

- First step toward enlargement

The goal of enlarging your tent isn't to seek self-glorification. Instead, it's about creating more space to receive and share God's blessings. When we align our growth with divine purpose, we become vessels through which the greater good can flow into the world.

Your enlarged tent awaits. Will you begin stretching today?

Chapter 23
Launch into the Deep

"Launch out into the deep, and let down your nets for a catch."
–Luke 5:4

I've reflected on this verse and story during my darkest moments of doubt, when effort feels useless and giving up seems like the only option left. It has always given me hope when I've reached the end of my strength and wondered: What now? When we realize we can't do it on our own and finally surrender to God's love and power, that's when He guides us to go deeper.

It was the morning after a long night. The tired fishermen cleaned their empty nets. Apostle Peter and the others had worked all night without catching anything—no fish, no income, just sore muscles and disappointed spirits. That's when Jesus appeared on the shore with this request: "Launch out into the deep and let down your nets for a catch."

I can picture the exhaustion and maybe frustration in Peter's voice when he said, "Master, we've worked hard all night and caught nothing." Still, something prompted him to add, "But because you say so, I will let down the nets." He decided to try again. What happened next was a miracle—the nets were so full of fish that they began to tear, requiring a second boat to hold all the fish.

"Launch out into the deep"

Jesus didn't tell the disciples to stay in the shallow waters where it was comfortable and safe. Instead, he directed them to go into the deep, where uncertainty rules, the water is darker, and you can't see the bottom, requiring complete trust in your vessel.

The deep represents that place beyond our comfort zones, beyond our calculated risks, and beyond what makes sense. It's the territory where faith becomes necessary because experience and logic alone won't carry you forward.

I've faced many invitations to go deeper throughout my life. Leaving my twenty-five-year corporate career, where I had achieved success. Starting a business, even when I was terrified of trying something new after so many years. Adjusting when COVID hit, a year after I left my job. Each time, the shallow waters of comfort seemed easier, promising me a false sense of safety but causing stagnation.

The deep is different for each of us. For some, it might mean pursuing a long-forgotten dream. For others, it could be having a difficult conversation or forgiving someone who seems unforgivable. For many, it's simply trusting God's voice when every external circumstance contradicts it.

"Let down your nets for a catch"

Jesus didn't just tell them to go into the deep. He instructed them to expect abundance there. This wasn't just about moving into uncertainty; it was about positioning themselves to receive what God had prepared.

The contrast is clear between working independently and taking action aligned with God. The disciples had been fishing all night, trying everything they could. But their nets stayed empty until they aligned their efforts with divine guidance. Their obedience to Jesus's call paved the way for the miracle that followed.

I believe that God honors both our faith and our willingness to act on it. Too often, we embody one without the other. We pray without stepping out, or we step out without seeking guidance. Peter and the other fishermen teach us that transformation happens through our faith and obedience working together, not by our effort alone.

There was a time in my life when I prayed for guidance while staying safely on shore. I wanted clarity before making a commitment. I needed guarantees before taking a risk. But the miracle was in the deep waters, not in my comfort zone's shallow waters. Only when I was willing to step out—take that uncertain leap—did the abundance appear.

When Exhaustion Meets Invitation

Perhaps the most interesting part of this story is its timing. Jesus didn't show up when the disciples were fresh and energized; he arrived when they were exhausted, discouraged, and ready to give up.

How often do we give up just before reaching the finish line? How close are we to achieving our goals, yet we stop short? Our flesh wants to quit. We want to see how it will turn out before we push further.

I used to get frustrated reading about how often the disciples repeated the same mistakes, even though they walked with Jesus every day. Now I see myself in their story. I forget what I've learned. I fall back into habits that don't help me. I try to do everything on my own until I'm exhausted, forgetting that God is ready to help. I am just like them.

As I write these words, I'm emerging from a few weeks of struggle, fighting with myself, my old patterns, and my self-sabotaging behaviors. I started this year exhausted, and instead of taking time to rest, I packed my schedule with meetings and work. I feel like I'm on a fast-moving train, and instead of figuring out how to get off, I keep holding on tighter. The answer is to let go, but I haven't.

This pattern is so deeply human. We push harder when we should let go. We pull back when we should move forward. We doubt when we should trust.

From Fishing to Following

The story doesn't end with the miraculous catch; that's just the beginning. When Peter saw the abundance, he fell to his knees in awe and unworthiness: "Go away from me, Lord; I am a sinful man!" But Jesus replied, "Don't be afraid; from now on, you will fish for people."

So, Simon, James, and John brought their boats ashore, left everything—including their entire catch—and followed Jesus. The miracle wasn't the end; it was the invitation to something greater. The abundance wasn't meant to satisfy their immediate needs; it was meant to reveal the provider.

My human curiosity wants to know more details. What happened to all those fish? Did they sell them first? Did they tell their families? The Scripture doesn't tell us because those details aren't the point. What matters is that an encounter with divine abundance completely changed their perspective and priorities.

The most significant transformation in this story isn't the empty nets becoming full; it's the fishermen becoming disciples. Their identity changed. Their purpose expanded. Their lives would never be the same because they went deeper in their faith.

This makes me wonder: What am I holding onto that God is asking me to let go of? What identity am I clinging to when He's offering something greater? What abundance am I pursuing when He's inviting me to seek Him instead?

The Beauty of Imperfect Faith

I love Peter because he reflects the messy reality of growing faith. He stepped out of the boat once, only to sink in fear another time. He called Jesus the Messiah, then tried to stop Him from completing His mission. He vowed never to deny Jesus, then did exactly that three times.

Yet this same imperfect Peter became the rock upon which Christ built His church. His story reminds me that transformation isn't about perfect performance but persistent return. When Peter fell, he got back up. When he failed, he returned to Jesus. Even when he doubted, he still showed up.

Our spiritual journey isn't a straight line of steady progress. It's a winding path filled with breakthroughs and setbacks, insights, confusion, courage, and fear. The disciples' story reminds me that I can be wonderfully human while pursuing a divine connection.

Your Invitation to the Deep

These practices are designed to help you identify where God might be calling you to step outside your comfort zone, physically experience the act of stepping out in faith, and assess your personal "shallow waters," "deep waters," and potential "catch." Remember, this isn't about perfect performance; it's about being willing to try again, even when you're exhausted, and trusting that God can turn your empty nets into abundant bounties.

1. Journal Prompt

In which area of your life is God calling you to "launch into the deep"?

What would it take for you to act in obedience and trust Him with the outcome?

Write down any fears or doubts you have, and ask God to give you the courage to move forward in faith.

2. Embodiment Exercise: Step Out in Faith

Stand with your feet together and take a few deep breaths to center yourself. Close your eyes and imagine the part of your life where you feel God prompting you to step out and take a risk.

Imagine Jesus standing before you, calling you to step into the deep. Move forward with one foot, representing your willingness to trust in faith. Hold that position for a few seconds, feeling the ground beneath your feet.

As you stand in the deep waters of faith, say aloud: "I am stepping out in obedience, trusting that God will lead me into a place of breakthrough and abundance."

Reflect on the action of taking a step. How does it feel to trust God in the unknown? How can you continue to move forward with His guidance?

3. Identify Your Deep Waters

Take some time to identify specifically:

- What are your "shallow waters"? (The comfortable, familiar places you tend to stay)
- What are your "deep waters"? (The places God may be calling you that feel frightening or uncertain)
- What "nets" do you need to let down? (Actions of faith you need to take)
- What "catch" is God preparing for you? (Blessings that could come from your obedience)
- What do you need to "leave behind" to follow more fully? (Things that may be holding you back)

Remember that Jesus called ordinary people, doing ordinary work, to witness extraordinary abundance, and then become something entirely new. Your story of transformation might start right where you are, with familiar challenges and daily struggles. But your willingness to go into the deep, to let down your nets one more time, sets you up for divine encounters that can completely change your journey.

The invitation to the deep awaits. Will you launch out today?

Chapter 24
Very Good Creation

"God saw all that he had made, and it was very good." –Genesis 1:31

I was standing in front of my bathroom mirror one morning, noticing every perceived flaw on my face and body, when suddenly this verse echoed in my mind: "God saw all that he had made, and it was very good."

Did you notice that? "It was very good." When God created the entire universe—with its endless galaxies, stunning mountains, vast oceans, and complex ecosystems—He didn't call it magnificent, glorious, spectacular, breathtaking, perfect, or amazing. He simply said it was "very good."

And you and I are part of that creation. Made in His image. Designed with intention. And, declared to be very good.

"God saw"

There's something profound about truly being seen. Not the superficial seeing that happens during fleeting encounters, but the deep, knowing gaze that perceives our true essence. God's seeing isn't just casual observation; it's His intimate understanding of every detail, every molecule, every thought, and every intention.

When the Creator of the universe looks at you, He doesn't see what you see in the mirror. He doesn't focus on the flaws you perceive or the mistakes you've cataloged. Instead, He sees His handiwork. His image bearer. His beloved creation.

I've spent countless hours trying to be seen differently—trying to appear more accomplished, more put-together, more worthy of approval. Yet, all along, I was already fully seen by the One whose opinion matters most.

"All that he had made"

Creation wasn't divided into sections. God didn't categorize His work as "exceptional," "adequate," or "needs improvement." The statement of "very good" covered everything He had made—including us humans, with all our complexity.

We are made in God's image, and He enjoys us and all His creation. Nothing more needs to be added or removed. We are valuable because He created us. We are part of His masterpiece.

So, why do I sometimes feel the need to be perfect or to make everything perfect? Why do I doubt my worth? What if I don't need to be anything more than who I was meant to be? What would it mean if I could let go of perfectionism?

Looking back at my journal entries, I declared that I was releasing perfectionism almost every week. I began to ask myself, "If perfectionism wasn't an issue, what would my life look like?"

I would be more open, share more of myself, and not hide who I am. I would show my face and share more of my life on social media. I would accept and take pride in my imperfections.

"It was very good"

Not perfect. Not flawless. Very good.

There is a big difference between aiming for excellence and being caught up in perfectionism. Excellence celebrates our talents and encourages us to use them well. Perfectionism sets an impossible standard that no one can achieve.

Journal Entry, May 15, 2020

Choosing FREEDOM over perfection.

I've become more aware of an affliction that many of us—including myself—share. It's our quest for perfection and high achievement. It's a striving, a daily challenge, an itch that we keep scratching. It's filling every minute of the day with activities to feel a sense of accomplishment as we cross them off the list. Not only is it exhausting, but perfectionism can cause procrastination, waiting for things to be perfect before they're finished, and not taking chances on new ideas for fear of judgment. What if we don't want perfection, but what we really need is FREEDOM?

Seeking to do something well is not the real problem—high standards and exceptional quality are admirable virtues. It is our pursuit of an unrealistic goal, the punishment we impose on ourselves if or when we miss the mark, and our fear of judgment from others that show this pursuit comes at a cost. We believe the stories that we have to be perfect. We wake up in the middle of the night thinking about our lists, fears, and failures. We convince ourselves that crossing things off our lists gives us a strong sense of accomplishment at the end of a productive day, but at what expense?

This journal entry marked a turning point in my journey—the moment I realized that my relentless pursuit of perfection wasn't bringing me closer to God or my true self. It was actually creating distance.

Perfectionism makes us believe we're never enough. Faith reminds us that we already are. Perfectionism focuses on appearance, while faith looks at the heart. Perfectionism demands control; faith surrenders to divine wisdom. Perfectionism lives in fear of failure, but faith finds purpose in the process.

Pathways to Freedom

What if we prioritized freedom over perfection? What would freedom look like in our everyday lives? Choosing freedom instead of perfection opens up more space for creativity, joy, and peace. Freedom helps us break free from the chains of self-imposed limits and encourages self-expression and growth. Perfection feels sharp and rigid, like a finely sharpened pencil. In contrast, freedom is flowing, lively, and playful.

It is not easy to suddenly decide to abandon our need for perfection. I've found that by making small changes daily, I can add more freedom, passion, and purpose to my life.

1. Embrace Creativity Without Judgment

Add more creativity to your life by sketching, coloring, drawing, writing, cooking, and baking. Try out hobbies just for fun. Choosing activities that can get messy helps you practice finishing tasks without needing perfect results.

The creative process demonstrates how God works in our lives—natural, growing, sometimes messy, but always filled with love. When we create without judgment, we connect with the Creator's heart.

2. Step Into Sacred Discomfort

Do something that scares you every day or try something you're not good at yet. It could be writing an article, posting a video, or trying a new activity. Decide what is "good enough" instead of waiting for everything to be perfect.

Trust me, it's not as scary as you think, and practicing what scares you more often will help the fear and worry fade away. Every time you choose growth over comfort, you're showing trust in the God who created you for more than just safety.

3. Practice Holy Simplicity

Remove unnecessary items and anything that doesn't bring joy from your daily list. Some things end up there because we feel the need to fill every minute with activity. It's okay and healthy to rest, think, and be fully present in the moment.

Remember that even God designed the Sabbath into the rhythm of creation. Rest isn't laziness; it's a sacred acknowledgment that our worth isn't linked to productivity.

4. Prioritize Divine Self-Care

Make self-care a priority in your daily to-do list. If you don't recharge your energy each day, you'll have nothing left to give to others. Include items that focus on your health, growth, development, happiness, and peace.

Taking care of your body, mind, and spirit isn't selfish; it's honoring the temple God has entrusted to you, through which His light shines into the world.

5. Align With Your True Purpose

Start saying "no" to things that don't matter and saying "yes" to things that align with your dreams. How often do we say "yes" because we feel like we should or because we don't want to disappoint those we care about? Other people's agendas shouldn't become your to-do list.

Your unique calling requires focus and intention. Every "no" to what doesn't align makes room for the divine "yes" that's waiting for you.

6. Celebrate Your Sacred Uniqueness

Stop comparing yourself to others. We each have a one in 400 trillion chance of being alive. Each of us has unique experiences, skills, talents, and interests. Focus on what makes you happy and start there.

Comparison is the thief of joy, but it also dishonors the specific way God designed you. Your path isn't meant to look like anyone else's—it's a one-of-a-kind journey between you and your Creator.

The Journey to "Very Good"

Looking back, the last time I wrote about perfectionism was in January 2023. I said, "The lesson was for me to push past perfectionism, to choose inward progress more than outward appearance, to not quit because something didn't turn out as expected, and to not make assumptions on others' behalf."

I was worried because I had a retreat planned at my house, and a burst pipe forced us to rip up part of the basement flooring. I covered the missing area with a rug, rearranged the furniture and tables, and explained what had happened to my guests... and no one cared. It wasn't about my floor; it was about me showing love and support to them on their journey.

This experience taught me that what I see as imperfections often go unnoticed by others. The flaws I fixate on are usually invisible to everyone else, and even if they aren't, they are minor compared to the importance of showing up authentically and with love.

Perfectionism robs us of joy. It convinces us we're not enough. Letting go of perfectionism and focusing on showing up authentically has brought me freedom, peace, and much more joy. It removed constraints and unlocked more creativity. It's allowed me to show up more often and in bigger ways in the world.

Saying we are "very good" isn't settling for mediocrity—it's embracing a divine standard that values wholeness over flawlessness, authenticity over appearance, and love over performance.

Your "Very Good" Practices

These practices are meant to help you embrace your identity as part of God's "very good" creation. They will guide you to imagine how your life could change if you truly believed in your inherent worth, physically feel what it's like to claim your dignity as God's child, and recognize where perfectionism might be stealing your joy and freedom. God didn't declare creation "perfect"; He called it "very good," giving us permission to release the heavy burden of flawlessness and accept our authentic, worthy selves.

1. Journal Prompt

Do you find it hard to recognize your worth? Do you struggle with perfectionism? What could happen if you let go of these thoughts and saw yourself as part of God's masterpiece? How would your daily life change if you truly believed you were "very good" just as you are?

2. Embodiment Exercise: Embrace Your Worth

Find a quiet place and sit or stand comfortably. Close your eyes and breathe deeply several times.

Imagine yourself as part of God's beautiful and good creation. Visualize being surrounded by His creation, knowing that you reflect His goodness.

Quietly tell yourself: "I am very good because I am created by God, in His image, and with a great purpose." Repeat this affirmation as you stand or move around, noticing the beauty of the world around you.

What is it like to realize your worth as part of God's perfect creation? How can you incorporate this sense of dignity into your daily life?

Every day offers a new beginning. While we can't control or choose all our circumstances, we can focus on actions that bring more peace, passion, purpose, and freedom into our lives. We can choose to see ourselves through God's eyes, as "very good" creations with inherent worth and a unique purpose.

The world constantly pushes you toward impossible standards of perfection. But divine wisdom guides you along a different path where you are already enough, worthy, and loved. Not because you've earned it through perfect performance, but because the One who created you declared it so from the beginning.

You are very good. Will you believe it today?

Chapter 25

Cultivating Good Soil

"A sower went out to sow. And as he sowed, some seeds fell along the path, and the birds came and devoured them. Other seeds fell on rocky ground, where they did not have much soil, and immediately they sprang up since they had no depth of soil, but when the sun rose, they were scorched. And since they had no root, they withered away. Other seeds fell among thorns, and the thorns grew up and choked them. Other seeds fell on good soil and produced grain, some a hundredfold, some sixty, some thirty. He who has ears, let him hear."
–Matthew 13:3–9

Since leaving my corporate career, I've spent more time planting flowers, herbs, and other plants around our home. I always envisioned having a beautiful outdoor space where my family and I could relax. One spring morning, as I was in my garden turning over the soil for planting, I thought of this parable. My hands were deep in the earth, breaking up compacted dirt, removing stones, and pulling weeds that had already started to sprout. I was preparing the soil.

I've heard this story and read it many times, but I wasn't sure what I needed to do personally for my own harvest. When the sower scattered his seeds, only those sown in fertile ground grew deep roots and produced abundance. I want to be that fertile ground, too. But how do we ensure we're ready to receive and nurture what God plants within us?

Understanding the Soil of Our Hearts

This parable isn't just about hearing God's Word; it's about how we receive it. The soil symbolizes the condition of our heart. Some hear the divine message, and it takes root deeply in their heart. Others listen to it, and their heart becomes hard, preventing anything from taking hold. We decide whether our hearts are open to God's Word and whether it produces fertile ground for spiritual growth.

Each type of soil in the parable represents a different heart condition:

The Path: The Hardened Heart

Seeds that fall on the path are quickly eaten by birds. The compacted soil prevents the seeds from taking root. Similarly, when our hearts become hardened by disappointment, cynicism, or constant busyness, divine wisdom cannot penetrate. The messages might reach our ears, but they don't truly sink into our being.

I recognize this hardened soil within myself when I go through life on autopilot, focusing so much on doing that I forget about being. In those seasons, I feel distant from God.

Rocky Ground: The Shallow Heart

Seeds that fall on rocky ground sprout quickly but wither just as fast because they can't develop deep roots. This is enthusiasm without commitment, spiritual excitement without the discipline to nurture growth.

I've noticed this happen every time I come across an inspiring message or spiritual insight, only to see my enthusiasm fade within days because I didn't make space for it to take hold in my daily life. Initial excitement without continual nurturing results in spiritual decline.

Thorny Ground: The Cluttered Heart

Seeds that fell among thorns were choked out by competing growth because this soil had potential, but it was already occupied by other priorities vying for resources.

This is the soil condition I struggle with the most: being busy, juggling too many priorities, and not taking the time to rest and listen.

My life can become so cluttered with commitments, worries, and distractions that even when divine wisdom takes root, it struggles to thrive amid everything demanding my attention. The thorns of anxiety, overconsumption, and endless to-do lists block the space needed for spiritual growth.

Good Soil: The Receptive Heart

Seeds that fell on good soil yielded a bountiful harvest. This soil was prepared—soft enough to receive, deep enough to develop roots, and clear enough to foster growth.

The moments when I have experienced the greatest spiritual growth in my life occurred when I intentionally prepared my heart through consistent practices that keep me open, clear, and receptive to divine guidance.

From Soil Maintenance to Abundant Harvest

I used to believe I had to work hard to earn it, but then I realized that my job is to nurture my soil's fertility through worship and spiritual discipline. I don't create the seeds or force them to grow; I just prepare the environment where growth can happen naturally.

Worship, meditation, prayer, silence, Scripture, and daily disciplines all help keep my vessel clean—my mind, body, and spirit. All of this is within my control. How I choose to show up each day affects how receptive my soil is to divine wisdom.

When I meditate, I become more present and mindful, which helps me hear God's voice more clearly. When I spend time in nature, I feel grounded, and I find it easier to come up with new ideas or gain greater clarity. When I eat healthy foods and limit substances that dull my awareness, I feel lighter and closer to God and nature.

I've realized that I feel the most anxious when I haven't asked God for help with my struggles. When I skip or bypass my spiritual practices to do more, work harder, and rely on my own strength, my heart becomes closed off and unreceptive. The seeds can't take root deeply in those conditions.

But when I am aligned and connected to God, I feel that anything is possible. The soil of my heart becomes rich with possibility, and what grows there nourishes not only me but those around me.

Dreams Planted in Fertile Soil

Journal Entry, January 20, 2024

Lord, I know You placed the vision and dream in my heart to give a TED Talk. I invite You to guide me through this process. Lead my choice of topic, direct my application, help me craft my stories, and guide my discipline in creating videos. Help me take notes today in class and stay attentive.

I invite you to bring clients who share my mission into my programs. I will promote, highlight, create content, and ask for the business, and I invite you to join as well.

I invite you into my creation. You are the creator, and I am the vessel. I do not want to do anything apart from you. I surrender my expectations to you. I seek your connection, alignment, guidance, and voice. I desire to feel you move within me—whether it's the flutter in my belly, the skip of a heartbeat, my Spidey senses, my intuition, or my thoughts. I aim to wake up each day worshiping you continuously, seeing the beauty all around me as you do, and appreciating your creation. I strive to always be grateful for what is right now, breathing and living through each moment. I want to catch glimpses of how you see me—perhaps a little more each day—so I don't retract or become small again. Thank you for stretching and refining me.

I know because you have shown me the future version of myself. I am in the best shape of my life, the healthiest I have ever been. I am healthy and confident in my beliefs. I am strong because I stand on solid ground, fertile soil, and remain tethered to You. I have a direct connection and line to You right now. I am emerging—like a butterfly being formed. It's the chrysalis or pupal stage—the transition phase. Maybe that's why I love butterflies so much.

I see myself on the TEDx stage giving my talk. I see myself as Your vessel. You are speaking through me, loving through me, communicating through me. I am traveling the world speaking, accompanied by Dorel. I am hosting retreats, writing books, and interviewing incredible people. I attract people who are ready to transform. They are prepared to grow. I see myself writing and publishing books that reach millions. I see myself coaching, inspiring, and giving people hope. I see myself sharing Your love for us. I do not have to do this alone. I am not here to struggle.

I align myself with Your vision of me, my God. I trust what You tell me. I am alive knowing that You are guiding my way, not me. How freeing and liberating that is. Thank You for pursuing me. Thank You for loving me. Thank You for holding me. Thank You for protecting me. Thank You for believing in me. I love You.

Reading this journal entry, I can tell I was deeply engaged in my spiritual practices that day. The soil of my heart was prepared and receptive, allowing divine dreams to take root.

My instinct still sometimes is to make myself small, to negotiate with my dreams and refine them to an "acceptable" size that won't risk disappointment or judgment. Then I remember that if the dream is in my heart, God placed it there. He will handle the how. I just need to stay aligned and connected to my Creator and take daily steps in that direction.

This is the sacred partnership of spiritual growth: I do my part by keeping my heart pure, open, receptive, and loving. God plants the seeds and nurtures the fruit. I can't force the growth, but I can create the right conditions for it to thrive naturally.

The Signs of Fertile Soil

How can we tell if our spiritual soil is healthy? I've identified several signs that help me gauge my heart's readiness to receive and cultivate divine wisdom.

Presence

When my soil is fertile, I fully embrace each moment instead of dwelling on the past or future. I notice details, appreciate beauty, and connect deeply with what's in front of me.

Receptivity

Fertile soil welcomes new insights and perspectives. When my heart is open, I find myself saying, "I hadn't thought of that," instead of dismissing ideas that challenge me immediately.

Resilience

Good soil doesn't wash away with the first rain. When my spiritual foundation is strong, challenges may shake me, but they won't uproot me. I can face difficulties with stability instead of a spiritual crisis.

Generosity

Abundant harvests naturally promote sharing. When my spiritual life flourishes, I become more generous with my time, resources, attention, and compassion.

Discernment

Healthy soil supports what should grow and reveals what shouldn't. When my heart is healthy, I can more easily tell authentic divine guidance from the many counterfeits vying for my attention.

Joy

Perhaps the clearest sign of fertile spiritual ground is joy that doesn't rely on circumstances. Not constant happiness, but a deep, lasting sense of delight in simply being alive and connected to the divine.

Practical Soil Cultivation

The great thing about this parable is that soil conditions can change. The path can be broken up, rocks can be removed, and thorns can be uprooted. Through consistent spiritual practices, even the most hardened hearts can become open to divine wisdom.

Here are some practical ways to cultivate the soil of your heart:

1. Create Sacred Space

Dedicate daily time to spiritual practices like prayer, meditation, Scripture reading, or contemplation. Even just ten to fifteen minutes of focused stillness can help soften even the hardest soil.

2. Practice Mindful Awareness

Throughout your day, take moments to notice where your attention is. Gently redirect it to the present when you catch yourself dwelling in worry, regret, or distraction.

3. Engage in Regular Self-Reflection

Take time weekly to examine the condition of your heart. What's taking up space? What needs to be uprooted? What needs more nurturing? Journaling can be a powerful tool for this reflection.

4. Cultivate Spiritual Community

Good gardeners share knowledge and support one another. Connect with others who are also caring for their spiritual soil, whether through a formal religious community or informal spiritual friendships.

5. Simplify Your Life

Identify clutter in physical, digital, mental, or emotional areas that may hinder your spiritual growth. Make space intentionally by minimizing what doesn't align with your highest purpose.

6. Connect with Nature

Spend time regularly outdoors in natural settings. The soil, plants, and natural cycles can act as powerful teachers and reminders of spiritual principles.

7. Practice Gratitude

Thankfulness softens the heart and invites more blessings. Daily acknowledgment of gifts, whether big or small, tills the soil of your spirit.

Your Good Soil Practices

I've created these practices to help you prepare the soil of your heart so divine wisdom can take root. They are designed to guide you in recognizing your personal habits that nurture the soil, physically experience what it feels like to remove obstacles to growth, and evaluate the current state of your spiritual soil in different areas of life. Your role isn't to force growth or plant the seeds; it's simply to maintain fertile conditions where what God plants can grow naturally and produce a bountiful harvest.

1. Journal Prompt

What practices help you cultivate healthy soil? Are there areas where you need to deepen your roots or soften your heart to allow God space to work? What specific steps can you take this week to improve the health of your spiritual soil?

2. Embodiment Exercise: Preparing the Soil of Your Heart

Find a quiet place where you can focus and think. Take a few deep breaths to clear your mind.

Imagine your heart as a patch of soil. Notice areas that might be hard, rocky, or filled with thorns. Visualize yourself tending to the soil by softening it, removing the rocks, and pulling out the weeds to make it fertile and prepared for new growth.

As you visualize, say to yourself: "I am preparing my heart to receive the Word of God and let it take root in my life. I will nurture it and allow it to bear good fruit."

What does it feel like to take active steps to prepare your heart for spiritual growth?

How can you continue to cultivate good soil in your life moving forward?

The parable of the sower reminds us that the same divine wisdom falls on all types of hearts, but only those who prepare themselves will experience its full transformative power. The condition of your soil isn't fixed—it can change through intentional practices and divine grace working together.

God generously scatters seeds of wisdom, purpose, and love. Our role is to ensure that when these seeds land, they find soil that welcomes, nurtures, and allows them to grow into something beautiful and nourishing.

Good soil doesn't develop overnight, nor is it sustained without steady care. But the harvest it yields—a life of purpose, peace, and divine connection—makes every moment of cultivation worthwhile.

Will you tend to your soil today?

Chapter 26

Double Portion

"'What can I do for you before I am taken from you?' Elisha answered, 'Please let there be a double portion of your spirit on me.'" –2 Kings 2:9

The first time I heard this Scripture in church, my heart skipped a beat, and it still does every time I read these words. Something about Elisha's bold request resonates deeply within my spirit, challenging me to examine the limits of my own faith and courage.

The prophet Elijah and his spiritual protégé Elisha stood by the Jordan River. Elijah knew he would soon be taken to heaven, completing his earthly mission. Before that happened, he took his cloak, rolled it up, and struck the water. Instantly, the river parted, creating a dry path for them to cross. After witnessing this miracle—one of many during their time together—Elijah turned to Elisha with a question that would change everything: "What can I do for you before I am taken?"

Despite witnessing the impossible and already following the greatest prophet of his time, Elisha's request was bold and daring: "Please let there be a double portion of your spirit on me."

The Audacity of Sacred Asking

How bold of Elisha to ask his mentor for a double portion! Even Elijah was surprised, unsure if his request could be granted: "You have asked a hard thing; yet, if you see me as I am being taken from you, it shall be so for you; but if you do not see me, it shall not be so" (2 Kings 2:10).

I believe Elijah was saying something profound—that if Elisha could see the spiritual reality of Elijah's transition, if his spiritual eyes were open enough to witness the supernatural chariot of fire that would take Elijah up to heaven, then his faith was strong enough to receive what he had asked for. The ability to see would be proof of his readiness to receive and serve.

This wasn't about Elisha's worthiness. It wasn't about whether he had earned the right to this spiritual inheritance. It was about his ability to receive it, and his spiritual eyes being open enough to see beyond the physical realm.

And yes, Elisha saw the chariot come for Elijah and watched as his mentor and prophet was taken to heaven. He picked up Elijah's fallen cloak, which was a physical symbol of the spiritual mantle he would now carry, and stepped into a new chapter of his calling. And guess what? During his lifetime, Elisha performed twice as many recorded miracles as Elijah. He received exactly what he had boldly requested—a double portion.

From Fear to Faith

I often think about what might have gone through Elisha's mind knowing his mentor was about to leave and he would be on his own. Elisha could have faced this transition with fear. He might have worried about losing his mentor, having to lead alone, and filling Elijah's shoes. Instead, he faced it with expectation and courage.

I'm surprised at how often we respond to big life changes with anxiety instead of excitement. I've done that, and I still do it, often. We focus on what we're losing rather than what we might gain. We settle for just getting through the change instead of thriving in it.

This story makes me reflect on my own life and whether I settle for comfort or choose to live boldly. Am I asking God for just enough to get by, or am I courageous enough to ask for abundance that could transform not only my life but also the lives of others?

I know I come from resilient roots. My great-grandfather on my father's side was a POW for three years after WWI and walked home to Serbia from Italy. During his three-month-long journey home, he survived on grass, corn from fields, and whatever sustenance he could find. My grandparents on both sides left Serbia for opportunities in Switzerland and the United States, sacrificing familiarity for the chance to provide better lives for their families. My parents and I immigrated to the States, where they built a new life from nothing.

With such proof of courage and faith in my lineage, why would I ask for anything less than a double portion? Why would any of us?

Defining Your Double Portion

The double portion I seek is deep alignment with God, peace, joy, health, faith, love, abundance, connection, creativity, curiosity, possibility, wisdom, and impact. I know that I am not here to live a small life, but to be the hands and feet of God. We all are.

For Elisha, the double portion appeared as miraculous signs of God's power. For us, it might take on a different meaning. Your double portion could mean:

- Twice the compassion your parents show
- A faith stronger than you've ever felt before
- Greater impact in your community than you ever imagined
- More abundant provision than what you've accepted
- Healing that reaches beyond yourself to your family lineage
- Wisdom surpassing human understanding
- Love that transforms not only your life but also the lives you touch

The specifics of your double portion will depend on your calling and circumstances. What matters is having the courage to ask for it, the faith to believe it's possible, and the willingness to steward it when it arrives.

Divine Partnership

I've wrestled with the question: Who determines how impactful our actions will be? Does God decide in advance, or is it a partnership between us and God that depends on our faith? Would Elisha have had the same influence if he hadn't asked, believed, and opened himself up to receive?

I've come to believe that while God's sovereignty is absolute, He has created spiritual growth as a partnership. Our faith, requests, and aligned actions all matter. They don't earn God's favor but help us receive what He already intends to give.

Imagine how this story might have turned out differently if Elisha had asked for something smaller.

- Please just let me survive without you.
- Please don't let the other prophets reject my leadership.
- Please give me just enough anointing to sustain what you've built.

Instead, he asked for a double portion and received it. Through his faith and aligned actions, the next step was set in motion for him. I believe the same applies to us. God invites us into co-creation, where our bold requests and faithful actions become the channels through which divine purpose unfolds.

This doesn't mean our requests limit God or that we can manipulate the divine through the right spiritual formulas. Instead, I believe that God has designed spiritual growth to involve our participation. Our asking matters, our beliefs matter, and our receiving matters.

The Responsibility of Receiving

Receiving a double portion isn't just about blessings—it's about responsibility. Elisha didn't ask for twice the comfort or twice the recognition. He asked for twice the spirit, knowing it would mean twice the work, twice the challenges, and twice the responsibility.

When we ask for more of God's Spirit, we seek to become more actively involved in His plans. We welcome greater challenges that will test our faith. We dedicate ourselves to facing whatever comes our way for the good of others, not just ourselves.

I'm still on my life's journey, and part of that involves letting go of everything I've accumulated that no longer serves me—old wounds, limiting beliefs, and generational patterns that restrict rather than empower. As I do this inner work, I think about Elisha's request. I want a double portion of blessings from my lineage. I seek to break the patterns and release the trauma while building on their courage, vision, resilience, and faith that God will protect and provide.

This is the beautiful paradox of the double portion—*it often requires letting go before gaining more.* Elisha had to release Elijah before receiving his mantle. We, too, may need to let go of what's familiar before stepping into a greater purpose.

Seeing Beyond the Visible

Remember Elijah's condition: "If you see me when I am taken from you, it shall be yours." Spiritual perception is the key to receiving the double portion.

In our lives, developing spiritual sight—the ability to see beyond physical limits, beyond conventional wisdom, and beyond what seems possible—is essential for receiving a greater measure of God's Spirit. This kind of seeing requires:

- **Regular communion with God** – Growing our spiritual senses through prayer, worship, and meditation
- **Studying sacred wisdom** – Immersing ourselves in Scripture and spiritual teachings
- **Practicing discernment** – Learning to distinguish between divine guidance and other voices
- **Living with expectancy** – Embracing each day with anticipation of divine encounters
- **Surrounding ourselves with a spiritual community** – Learning from others who notice what we might overlook

When we develop spiritual sight, we become more aware of divine actions. We notice invitations we might otherwise miss. We perceive possibilities that are invisible to those who focus solely on material reality.

Elisha saw the chariots of fire because he had spent years honing his spiritual perception under Elijah's mentorship. His eyes were ready to see beyond the veil when the crucial moment arrived.

Your Double Portion Practices

I've created these practices to help you embrace your double portion with faith and courage. They will guide you in recognizing your specific double-portion request, physically experiencing what it feels like to receive and step into a spiritual mantle, and understanding what increased capacity could look like in different areas of your life. This isn't about selfishly demanding blessings—it's about courageously asking for greater spiritual capacity to fulfill your divine purpose and serve others more effectively.

1. Journal Prompt

If you were as bold, courageous, and faithful as Elisha, what kind of impact could you have on this world? What is your double-portion request? Are you ready to step into a new level of leadership, faith, and responsibility? What is your mantle?

2. Embodiment Exercise: Stepping into Your Mantle

Find a quiet space and take deep breaths. Close your eyes and visualize Elijah passing the mantle to Elisha.

Imagine a mantle being placed on your shoulders. What does it feel like? Is it heavy, light, warm?

Speak this affirmation aloud: "I am ready to step into my calling. I receive what God has prepared for me."

Take a physical step forward. As you do, imagine yourself stepping into your double portion—your next level of journey with God.

The story of Elisha shows that spiritual growth often begins with the courage to ask for more than what seems reasonable. It then requires faith to believe it's possible and culminates in the willingness to take on greater responsibility when the opportunity arises.

Your double portion is waiting for you. Not because you've earned it, but because God delights in increasing your ability to receive and share divine love. The question isn't whether God is willing to give more, but whether we're brave enough to ask, faithful enough to believe, and ready to receive.

I want to be as bold as Elisha. I pray to be as courageous and faithful. And I invite you to join me in this sacred audacity—asking not only for what we need, but for what will empower us to serve divine purpose more effectively in the world.

Will you ask for your double portion today?

LIVING IN LOVE

Chapter 27

The Greatest Commandment

"'Thou shalt love the Lord thy God with all thy heart, and with all thy soul, and with all thy strength, and with all thy mind; and thy neighbor as thyself.' Jesus then tells the scholar, 'Thou hast answered right: do this, and thou shalt live.'" –Luke 10:25–28

The Heart of All Faith

I haven't always identified as a religious person, but I am someone who loves Jesus deeply and wants to follow Him and His teachings. My faith is and has always been a personal relationship with my Savior. I included this verse because, according to Jesus, it's the most important and, I believe, the hardest to follow.

Many of us are familiar with the Ten Commandments in the Old Testament and know they serve as the laws Moses shared with God's people. In the book of Luke, a scholar asked Jesus, "What must I do to inherit eternal life?"

Instead of a list of rules and laws to follow, Jesus told the man to seek God first, to love God with all his heart, soul, strength, and mind—and to love others as much as he loves himself. If we eliminated all the rules and traditions of religion, we would be left with this core commandment: *Love God fully, and love others as yourself.*

Then Jesus tells him, "Do this, and you will live." Action is necessary for this verse to come alive. Not just knowing it, but embodying it. And this is where I know I fall short every day.

This commandment shifts our spiritual focus from merely following rules to building relationships. The scholar wanted to know the requirements, rules, or laws that one must obey to inherit eternal life. And as He often does, Jesus redirects us toward love instead. Because when we love God and our neighbors as ourselves, we naturally fulfill the other requirements. We instinctively live as we are meant to.

The difficult part is that we don't always love fully. We sometimes love God only on Sundays at church, when things go our way, or during certain spiritual practices. We may love some people, but not everyone. Those most like us are usually easier to love. We tend to overlook or dismiss others. The cancel culture has become so common because it's easier to cancel someone than to seek understanding and try to love them.

Maybe we don't love others because we judge ourselves too harshly and lack compassion for ourselves, leaving nothing to give, especially to those we dislike. "Love thy neighbor as thyself." Maybe we're trying to follow that, but we don't truly love ourselves.

We are unkind when we forget our inner divinity, our connection to God, and the fact that we are unconditionally loved. We neglect the fruits of the Spirit—love, joy, peace, patience, kindness, goodness, faithfulness, gentleness, and self-control. Maybe we can love our neighbors better by loving ourselves more, and that's tough work.

What Does Whole-Hearted Love Look Like?

I've spent many hours reflecting on what it means to love God with all my heart, soul, strength, and mind. This kind of love and devotion is all-encompassing and always present. While I love God deeply and feel my affection when I pray, read His Word, worship, see my kids, watch a sunset, and breathe in the ocean air, I also recognize that I fall short every day.

When my heart aligns with God, I find myself loving what He loves and caring about what He cares about. This kind of love involves surrender and seeking deeper alignment. When I love God with my soul, I surrender my plans, dreams, ambitions, and desires to His divine guidance. It's about trusting in God's will, not my own. It's about trusting His understanding, not mine. It's about allowing myself to be guided instead of trying to control circumstances.

Loving God with all my strength activates my faith, allowing me to trust that God will guide me. It's how I choose to use the gifts, skills, and experiences He has given me to honor Him. This is where my faith becomes visible to others through the way I serve, how I show up, and how I demonstrate my faith and beliefs.

Loving God with all my mind means using my intellect, creativity, and discernment for the greater good. It involves setting boundaries for what I allow into my life—what I consume and share.

While this verse may deliver a straightforward message that's easy to understand, putting it into practice is much harder. It might be simpler to follow a set of rules and check off the boxes, but that's not what He said.

Love as Transformation

Journal Entry, November 4, 2020

God spoke to me clearly during meditation this morning. He reminds me that the world will change when we change. The work has always focused on the internal first, then sharing externally. It won't happen through unkind words, arguments, or constantly trying to be right. It will not work by enforcing fear, but instead by choosing love. Jesus said that the greatest commandment is to love thy neighbor as thyself. Do unto others as you would have them do unto you.

So, the day after the election, we'll focus on clearing out things that block our energies, releasing attachments that don't serve us, and filling them back up with love rather than fear. Release resistance and accept the flow of life. Believe that all things happen for us, not to us. Let go of our ties to outcomes, be ready to go with the flow of life, whatever happens, and be part of the change we want to see.

I hope this morning's meditation class was healing. I hope it was received as I intended. I don't want to get political or make anyone uncomfortable. I want to share what I feel I'm supposed to share with others.

Today, I will pray that my work is filled with love, focus, and positive intention. I will pray before I begin and invite God, the Master Creator, to be my co-creator.

When I teach a meditation class and I don't recognize the words as ones I've chosen, I feel lost in the moment and trust that God is working through me. I guess for those who aren't spiritual, that sounds crazy—maybe even irresponsible or lazy. I don't see it that way. I could never plan to do something better than when I get lost in the flow, and the words come through me but aren't of me.

For me, loving others means listening, being kind, and inspiring with all my communications. It means sharing what benefits or helps others. It is to be the light that others need.

The Challenge of Love

Although the instructions may seem straightforward, applying them can be difficult. Online, we often see not only a lack of love for our neighbors but sometimes even hatred. Wars continue in many parts of the world, along with violence in our own homes and schools. We also experience hatred toward ourselves in our thoughts, the words we speak inwardly, and the choices we make. We are afraid to discuss our faith or our love for our Creator openly. We may not even know our neighbors well enough to love them genuinely.

How do we revisit this verse today? Each of us must find our own answer.

How do I love God with all that I am? It began with dedicating more time to daily devotion. I established morning rituals and routines that let me spend quiet moments with God. I read devotionals and spiritual texts. I breathe, meditate, practice gratitude, and pray. I listen to uplifting music and write. I call this my *Date with the Divine*. I do this every day, not just on Sundays or when I'm in trouble.

I look forward to this part of my day more than anything else. When I spend time with God in the morning, I feel a closer connection to Him. I talk to God, listen, and experience such a strong feeling of love and connection that it's undeniable. My heart fills with gratitude and an overwhelming sense of unconditional love, peace, and joy. Jesus showed us how to love others. From this place, I can pour into my clients. I believe that if I do this, they will feel it.

The Revolution of Divine Love

The greatest commandment invites us into a love that transforms everything. When we love God with our entire being and extend that same love to others, we're not just following a rule—we participate in divine life itself.

I've realized that this commandment is fulfilled not through effort but through surrender. As I get closer to God and seek to receive His love each morning, I become a conduit rather than a source. My own effort doesn't create the love I give to others, but it flows naturally from my connection with God.

This is how eternal life begins now—not as a future reward but as a present reality when we align with love's transformative power. By loving God fully, ourselves honestly, and others compassionately, we discover what Jesus promised: "Do this, and thou shalt live."

Your Love Practices

I've created three exercises to help you embody the greatest commandment in your daily life. These practices will guide you in recognizing where loving fully is most difficult, physically experiencing what it feels like to receive God's love, and then extending that love to others. They will also help you identify areas where your ability to love might be blocked or limited. This isn't about perfectly following religious rules—it's about engaging in divine life itself as you learn to love God with your whole being and extend that same love to yourself and others.

1. Journal Prompt

Do you love God with all your heart, soul, strength, and mind, and love your neighbor as yourself? What is the hardest part for you? What devotional practices can you develop to support your journey?

2. Embodiment Practice: The Love Flow Meditation

Find a comfortable spot to sit quietly. Close your eyes and take slow, deep breaths.

Place your hand on your heart and feel its steady beat. As you breathe in, imagine God's love filling you.

Speak this affirmation aloud: "God deeply loves me. I open my heart to love Him fully and to love others as He loves me."

Extend your arms outward. Visualize love flowing from your heart to the people in your life—family, friends, strangers, even those you find challenging to love.

Finish with gratitude. Thank God for His love and for the ability to share it with the world.

3. Love Assessment

In your life, reflect on:

- How fully do you express love?
- What blocks or limits your passion?
- What one practice might help you expand your capacity to love?
- What would change if you loved more fully in this dimension?

Remember that loving God and others isn't about following rules or earning spiritual points. It's about genuinely coming alive through connection with God, ourselves, and our neighbors. When we align our hearts with divine love, we become vessels through which this transformative power can flow into a hurting world.

The revolution of divine love is awaiting us. Will you start loving today?

Chapter 28

The Fruits of the Spirit

"But the fruit of the Spirit is love, joy, peace, patience, kindness, goodness, faithfulness, gentleness, and self-control." –Galatians 5:22

This verse has served as both a guide and a barometer for me. I assess my energy daily to see if it aligns with the fruits of the Spirit. For those familiar with the energetic vibrational frequency chart, the fruits of the Spirit are placed at the top. There are days when I wake up feeling energized and fully aligned, and others when I wake up anxious, worried, and scattered.

When Paul shared this verse, he was writing to the churches in Galatia, a region that is now part of modern-day Turkey. There was a conflict within the church between the Gentiles, who believed they had to follow all Jewish laws—including the tradition of circumcision—to become followers of Christ. Paul emphasized that salvation comes through faith in Jesus alone, not through works or obedience to the old law.

Cultivating Divine Qualities

He shares the fruits of the Spirit here and reminds them that these are signs of the Spirit within us. They reflect the nature of God and symbolize our spiritual growth. Growth and progress don't happen overnight and can't be forced, but they can be cultivated through our connection to God and His Word.

When I am my best self, I am loving, joyful, peaceful, patient, kind, good, faithful, gentle, and have self-control and discipline. When I am stressed, I exhibit the opposite qualities: I become fearful, anxious, impatient, and unkind in my words and thoughts, often losing control of my emotions. That's when I react from my ego, my earthly body, rather than from my Spirit. I recognize this, dislike it, and still struggle like many of us do. Our lives and how others perceive us reflect the nature of our spirit.

Spiritual Awakening

Journal Entry, March 26, 2021

I am awake! I've had a spiritual awakening. I listened to Rabbi David Aaron speak at one of Cathy Heller's bonus events, and everything finally made sense. I think I "knew" this before, but now I remember it as TRUE. We, our souls, who chose to come down as a piece of God, a part of the whole—like Jesus—to Earth. We took on physical form and agreed to live this life so we can become God personified on Earth. Jesus is our example. I am revisiting the Book of John again before Easter. Jesus said He came down not to dismantle the laws of the Old Testament but to fulfill them.

In *The Four Agreements*, Ruiz explains that when we sin, we harm ourselves. We cause ourselves grief because we are part of God. The Bible states that sin grieves the Holy Spirit, who dwells within us. This means that when we sin, we hurt ourselves, leading to feelings of guilt and shame.

Jesus often said He came to save, not to condemn. He forgave people for missing the mark and encouraged them not to sin again. Not as punishment, but because repeating the same choices that cause us illness, grief, pain, shame, and guilt keeps us stuck in those feelings instead of allowing God's light to work through us to do His work.

What does this mean for me? I want to emulate Christ here on earth. My purpose is to share love, tell people they are loved, show them they are divinely created, and teach what God has revealed to me about how to live. God is limitless and abundant; therefore, I am too. There is no linear time, no lack, no scarcity—only abundance.

My role is to do my part—create, write, teach, share, and love people. God will provide the opportunities, and I will fulfill my part. God will figure out how. I will stay grateful, alert, and alive. All of this is happening within me. It's not just a mental understanding but a knowing I feel deep in my heart, spirit, and soul. I can't fully explain how it all works, but the more I move forward, the more I feel whole, complete, peaceful, calm, fulfilled, and passionate when I embody the light and let my light (God) shine through me. More of God and less of the ego, false identity, and earthly feelings—none of which are truly God.

The veil has been lifted. I need to re-read everything. I want to explore more spiritual texts. I want to see how these messages connect and what more I can learn about God's nature and His message to us. But then I am reminded that God told us that He speaks to us in the still, quiet voice of our Soul. He is still speaking. He is still sharing.

Everything takes on new meaning. Avoid creating false idols—you cannot make an idol of God—God is a limitless light. All is energy—yes, because God is everywhere. Strive to be more like God (His energies, His choices, His feelings, His behaviors, etc.), and that's what we'll attract back to ourselves. When we become more like God, He draws closer to us as well. When we dwell on thoughts, dreams, or images that are not of God, we drift farther from Him and attract more of the same.

God is love and pure light; we cannot find Him if we cling to something else. If we stay in darkness, we will become more lost and confused. The first thing we do when entering a dark room is turn on the light. God, the Holy Spirit, is that light. We always have access to the light. When we ignite the flame within us, it shines outward and into a dark world. I have spoken these words before to my meditation group. Oh, Lord, thank you for being so patient with me. I cannot turn back now.

The other thought I had this morning is that if I chose to come into this body, this life, and these circumstances, I must be brave and confident in God's love. I feel like I came to break the cycle, the trauma, the violence, the addiction, and the fear, and to magnify God. I have family members of faith who were also seekers, but also people with deep human trauma. Trauma is what grieves the Spirit so deeply because it is so far from God and His love. Trauma inflicts pain and emotions not of God. It causes people to seek protection instead of liberation. I seek enlightenment and freedom from the flesh, from fears, and limitations.

How should I parent differently? I need to remind my children that they carry God within them. I should also remind them that drawing closer to God amplifies His goodness and power. God is powerful because He is pure LOVE, and love is the greatest of all emotions.

I'm feeling chills all over my body right now. I am healing. I am shedding. I am magnifying God. God, use me each day to do Your work.

Daily Devotion

Re-reading these entries is a gift. I am so grateful that I have been writing regularly. God has, is, and will continue to support us. The fruits are not something we work hard to earn; we do the work to be open to receiving them.

I know that becoming the best version of myself requires daily devotion and discipline. This includes waking up early, reading from Scripture or other texts, meditating, breathing, practicing gratitude, praying, and communicating with God through writing. These practices align me with God and, in turn, with the fruits of my Spirit.

Fruit That Ripens from Within

Remember that the fruits of the Spirit are natural results of a life connected to the divine. We can't force these qualities through effort; we naturally develop them when we stay rooted in God's presence.

Take a moment to imagine these fruits ripening inside you—love in your interactions, joy despite challenging moments, peace settling over your anxious thoughts. Feel how gentleness softens your approach to others, how patience broadens your ability to slow down, and how kindness reflects in your interactions.

Your Spiritual Fruit Practices

Below, you'll find three practices to help you nurture the fruits of the Spirit in your daily life. These will guide you in recognizing which spiritual disciplines bring you closer to your divine nature, experiencing these qualities through mindful movement, and evaluating which fruits may need more attention and care.

1. Journal Prompt

What practices help you grow closer to the fruit of your Spirit? Which fruit do you feel God is developing in you right now? Where do you see proof of His work in your life?

2. Embodiment Exercise: Walking in the Spirit

Practice breathwork by taking deep, steady breaths, inhaling through your nose and exhaling through your mouth. Inhale peace and exhale anything that doesn't serve you. Repeat this practice as needed.

Take a mindful walk outside and think about each fruit of the Spirit. As you move forward, say them aloud. Feel God's presence with each step. Picture yourself walking in harmony with the Spirit, letting these qualities deepen within you.

Finish your practice with gratitude, thanking God for the fruit He is cultivating in you, and seek His guidance to deepen your growth.

3. Fruit Assessment

For each fruit of the Spirit, consider:

- How naturally does this quality flow from you right now?
- What usually blocks or hinders this fruit in your life?
- What one practice could help you develop this fruit more fully?
- How could your relationships change if this fruit were more plentiful?

Remember that the fruits of the Spirit aren't qualities we try to develop through willpower or effort. They're natural results of a life connected to God.

The beauty of spiritual fruit is that it develops naturally. We don't need to force or fake it. Our job is simply to create the right conditions for growth through daily connection with the divine, and then trust the Holy Spirit to produce what we cannot produce on our own.

Will you tend to your spiritual garden today?

Chapter 29

A Heart of Gratitude

"It is good to give thanks to the Lord, and to sing praises to Your name...to declare Your loving kindness in the morning, and Your faithfulness every night." –Psalm 92:1–2

One of my favorite prayers is saying "Thank you" to God. It is such a simple prayer, yet every time I say it, my eyes fill with tears, my heart swells, and my throat trembles with emotion. I am humbled each time I give thanks because I see evidence of how supported, cared for, and loved I am and always have been. I recognize the deep privilege of my life and have committed to never taking God's abundant blessings for granted. I've learned over time that when I start and end my day with prayer, praise, and gratitude, I stay focused on what's important and become less distracted by the chaos in the world.

The Power of Appreciation

This Psalm is titled "A Song for the Sabbath" and was intended to be sung during worship. We believe King David wrote it and expresses gratitude for God's blessings and faithfulness to His people.

It's easy to forget to appreciate what is here right now. I know I'm guilty of pushing for more, working toward the next goal, and striving for what's next. I sometimes take for granted the things I already have. I don't slow down enough to celebrate how far I've come on my journey.

When I practice gratitude, I begin by appreciating basic needs that many people lack: access to clean drinking water, food, shelter, a bed, clothing, health, the ability to breathe, and to move. I give thanks for our health, my loving family, friends, a life I enjoy, the freedom to do what I love, travel, experience new things, keep my loved ones close, worship freely, and more.

I could spend days feeling grateful, and I still wouldn't reach the end because the more I appreciate what I have and give thanks, the more God reveals to me. Being in a state of gratitude opens our hearts to compassion, service, and love. We are kinder and more generous when we recognize what we have. Instead of fixating on what we want, focusing on what we already possess shifts our perspective.

Gratitude Throughout the Day

I believe that's why this Psalm says, "A day that begins and ends in prayer and praise won't become unraveled." I start my day by giving thanks before I open my eyes while I'm lying in bed.

Before my feet hit the floor, I thank God for another day, a good night's sleep, my cozy bed, my family nestled in theirs, and the chance to be God's hands and feet once again today.

I give thanks when I sip my first cup of coffee.

I give thanks when I read from the book that He wrote with me.

I give thanks when I write in my planner for the clients who have trusted me with their journeys.

I give thanks when Dorel joins me, and we read Scripture together for God's Word.

I give thanks when I co-create with God in the morning when we write.

I give thanks when I worship, breathe, pray, and meditate.

I give thanks when I teach my clients.

I give thanks when I have meals with my family.

I give thanks on my morning walk as I appreciate His majestic creation.

I give thanks when I turn on the bath or shower and can clean myself with hot water.

I give thanks when I read books and listen to podcasts that fill me with knowledge and truth.

I give thanks when I receive a text or call from a friend or family member.

I give thanks when I hear music that moves me to tears.

I give thanks for resting in the evenings.

I give thanks continuously as I walk around my house and appreciate this gift.

I give thanks as I prepare to sleep for the day's gifts.

Swimming in Abundance

Journal Entry, December 3, 2023

Thank you. Thank you. Thank you. I am truly grateful for all my blessings. I recognize that I am constantly receiving blessings. I receive them each time I wake up, breathe, and see the beauty around me as God channels His words through me. I receive them whenever I have the chance to serve. Every time I turn on the faucet, I get water; when I open the fridge, I have food; I shower, use my credit cards, utilities, watch TV, travel, use my phone, and wear clothes.

I receive from God all the time. I am swimming in abundance. I am swimming in love. I am swimming in provisions. I am swimming in blessings. I am swimming in overflow. I am swimming in joy. I am swimming in your blessings. There is overflow in my life right now. My family is healthy and alive. We have a home. We meet our needs and have extra. We have sound minds. We are together. We are able-bodied. We are swimming, swimming, swimming in abundance.

My tears are overflowing. I worship you, Lord. Thank you for always opening my eyes to what is already here. I am grateful and appreciative of what already exists. It's time to serve, donate, and do more to show my appreciation for what you've already done for me. Thank you. Thank you. Thank you.

Living in Gratitude

Living with a heart full of gratitude is living with more joy, love, compassion, and contentment.

Starting a gratitude practice is easy.

Morning: Before you wake, take a few minutes to express gratitude.

Midday: Give thanks for your meals.

Evening: Reflect on the day's blessings and name at least three things you're most grateful for.

Over time, you'll find yourself in a state of perpetual gratitude.

The Transformative Power of Thank You

Remember that gratitude isn't just a kind spiritual practice—it's a powerful force that changes how we experience life. When we train our eyes to notice the blessings around us instead of focusing on what's missing, everything shifts. Our problems might not disappear, but they are seen differently within the context of God's abundant provision and faithfulness.

Take a moment to pause and notice what is already in your life. Feel the air filling your lungs, the support of where you're sitting, and the miracle of your mind that can understand these words and find new meaning in them. These aren't small things—they're extraordinary gifts that we've simply become used to receiving.

The beautiful paradox of gratitude is that it both reminds us of our dependence on God and enables us to live more fully. When we view everything as a gift rather than an entitlement, we approach life with wonder instead of expectation, and with joy instead of demand.

Will you begin your own practice of gratitude today?

Your Gratitude Practices

The following practices will help you develop a grateful heart in your daily routine. They'll guide you to express thankfulness to God through writing, feel gratitude with each breath you take, and recognize when you might be taking blessings for granted. As you practice these exercises, notice how shifting your focus to appreciation instead of lack begins to change your entire experience of life.

1. Journal Prompt

What's your gratitude practice? Write a gratitude letter to God and thank Him. See what flows from you.

2. Embodiment Exercise: The Gratitude Breathwork Practice

Find a quiet spot and sit comfortably with your feet on the ground or in a relaxed position with your legs crossed underneath you.

Inhale deeply through the nose, saying in your mind: "Thank You, God, for this breath."

Exhale slowly, saying: "I trust You, Lord, with today."

Repeat for a few minutes, focusing on gratitude with each breath.

End by bringing your hands into a prayer position in the center of your chest and say, "Thank you."

3. Gratitude Assessment

- What specific blessings do you sometimes overlook or take for granted?
- How might intentional gratitude transform your experience in life?
- What one practice might help you cultivate more gratitude?
- How might expressing gratitude change your relationship with God?

The purpose of gratitude isn't about self-satisfaction or just positive thinking. Instead, it's about developing a heart that's open to receiving and sharing God's blessings. When we align our thankfulness with divine purpose, we become vessels through which His goodness can flow more freely into the world.

Your grateful heart awaits. Will you begin expressing gratitude and being thankful today?

Chapter 30

No More Separation

"His final piercing cry received an echoing response from the temple: Behold, the curtain was torn in two, from top to bottom. And the earth shook, and the rocks were split. The tombs also were opened."
–Matt 27:51

Every time I read a verse or passage, I tend to see something a little different, a new meaning, or it reminds me of something that is happening currently in my life or the world. I think that's one of the reasons why it's so important for me to read scripture regularly.

When I recently reread this verse, I was reminded that the veil that tore represented our separation from God. When it tore, Jesus was telling us that we have direct access to God through His sacrifice.

I looked up the definition of separation, and one meaning is the division of something into parts or elements. It made me think about the current division in our country and around the world. We see this separation everywhere—in polarized politics, fractured communities, and even within families. People cling tightly to their beliefs and identities, sometimes willing to cut ties with family, friends, and colleagues over political disagreements and contentious issues. Earlier this year, Minnesota Senator Melissa Hortman and her husband were killed at their home, and this week, someone murdered Charlie Kirk on a college campus where he was speaking. Both incidents are suspected to be politically motivated. How have we become so divided as a nation and as individuals?

The energy around separation is rarely neutral; it is usually filled with anger, defensiveness, and fear. We often fail to see ourselves as parts of the whole—eternal spiritual beings created by God who will each return to God. We forget that part of the spiritual journey here on Earth is to remember who we are, where we came from, and why we're here. If we believed that we are not separate, would we also remember to love, be kinder, compassionate, generous, and forgiving?

The Torn Veil

Can you imagine what it must have felt like to witness the moment the veil was torn? This passage describes one of the most significant events in spiritual history. The temple veil wasn't just any curtain—it separated the Holy of Holies, where it was believed that God's presence dwelled, from the rest of the temple. This space was so sacred that only the high priest could enter once a year on the Day of Atonement, carrying blood from a sacrifice to atone for the people's sins. No one else could enter this place.

Then came that moment on the cross. When Jesus gave up his spirit, the earth shook, and that heavy, thick veil tore completely—from top to bottom—symbolizing that there is no longer a separation between God and us.

We no longer need anyone else to connect with our Creator. We don't need to sacrifice animals or go through a priest to talk to God. Jesus became the ultimate, perfect sacrifice. God literally removed the barrier by sacrificing a part of Himself so we could know Him intimately, just like Adam and Eve did in the garden.

It's easy to assume Adam and Eve weren't real and that their story is just a myth. But what if it happened exactly as written? If it did happen as described, it's heartbreaking. Imagine being created to walk in perfect harmony with God, constantly in communion with your Creator, lacking nothing, living in paradise. They only had one rule—don't eat from the Tree of Knowledge of Good and Evil.

I used to struggle with this part of the story. Why wouldn't God want them to have knowledge? That seemed unfair until I realized that maybe it wasn't about withholding beneficial information. What if this "knowledge" was an awareness that would fundamentally change their existence, forever transforming how they, and we, experienced life and God?

Have you ever learned something so devastating that you wished you could forget it? Or seen something so traumatic that the image kept haunting you?

I believe that's what happened when they ate the fruit. It wasn't about gaining wisdom—it was about losing innocence. Suddenly, they became aware of their nakedness, something that had never caused shame before. They hid from the God they once freely walked with. The idea of shame didn't even exist in their minds until that moment. Their entire relationship with God, themselves, and each other changed instantly.

Spiritual Death

When Adam and Eve disobeyed God, they faced something more devastating than physical death. They created spiritual separation from their Creator. Suddenly, they could no longer walk and talk face-to-face with God as they had done every day. The moment they ate from that tree, their eyes opened to good and evil, and shame entered their consciousness for the first time.

Doesn't this pattern seem familiar in our own lives? When we do something we know isn't aligned with our higher selves, shame sneaks in, and what's our first response? We hide. We withdraw. We create distance from those we've hurt or disappointed, especially God. Our shame builds walls that separate us from love and connection.

How traumatic this must have been for Adam and Eve. One day, they were in close communion with the Creator of the universe, feeling His love surround them—and the next, they were cast out into a harsh new reality of pain and struggle. The garden wasn't erased from their memories; they carried the knowledge of what they'd lost.

Imagine remembering perfect peace and harmony while living in a world now filled with hardship, knowing your choices led to this new reality. It's heartbreaking to know paradise and peace and realize your actions caused a life of suffering. This pattern of separation continues through generations.

But then Jesus arrived. When He surrendered His spirit on the cross, the veil was torn—a divine sign that separation was over. We now have direct access to God—no intermediaries, no complex rituals, and no special class of people needed to approach Him. We can speak directly to the Creator of the universe, worship Him, seek His guidance, and understand His Word through the Holy Spirit living inside us. We are called to live by grace.

What does this mean for how we should live? Does it call us to shift our perspective and reevaluate our relationship with God? Are we actually co-creating our lives and existence right now?

Living in the Garden Again

What would it be like to live in the garden again? Imagine being in direct connection and harmony with God, where conversations with Him feel as natural as breathing. Picture a life where all our basic needs are not only met but generously provided for. Feel a deep sense of peace and a perfect, symbiotic relationship with nature. Envision a harmonious bond with the natural world—honoring creation with reverence, taking only what we need, and living with gratitude instead of endless consumption.

Imagine our relationships flourishing as we treat each other with kindness, love, understanding, forgiveness, and compassion. Perhaps the most challenging of all, we would release our desperate grip on control—that same desire shown in the Tree of Knowledge. Our need to be in charge, to choose our own way apart from God's wisdom, persists even when everything we need is already given.

Isn't this exactly what God wanted for Adam and Eve? He invited them to rest in their relationship with Him rather than seek independence and self-reliance. The moment they ate from that tree, their minds filled with harmful thoughts and feelings. They were still in the garden. What surprises me sometimes is that they remained there and in God's presence. Everything they needed was still around them. Yet their perception had changed profoundly, clouded by shame, fear, and doubt where there had once been only clarity and trust.

Isn't this how we live? We try to control everything, convinced we must figure it all out on our own. We struggle and suffer when the easier path—trusting our connection with God—seems out of reach. Maybe the torn veil calls us back to that garden-like relationship, not physically, but spiritually, reminding us that the separation was never God's idea in the first place.

Your Love Without Separation Practices

These practices will help you experience life without the veil of separation between you and God. They will guide you to visualize what reconnection could look like in your daily life, physically feel what it means to move from separation into divine presence, and identify any barriers that might still exist in your relationship with God. As you engage with these exercises, remember that the veil has already been torn; you are simply awakening to a connection that already exists.

1. Journal Prompt

What would life be like without a separation from God and your fellow humans? What would change? How can you strengthen your connection to God? Write about a time when you felt closest to God—what elements were present that you can incorporate into your daily life?

2. Embodiment Exercise: Crossing the Threshold

Find a doorway in your home or outside. Stand on one side of it, imagining the veil before you.

Close your eyes and take a deep breath. Think about anything that has made you feel distant from God—maybe shame, fear, guilt, or doubt.

Step through the doorway and quietly say, "No more separation." Visualize yourself completely entering God's grace and presence.

Pause on the other side. Feel the freedom of knowing you are completely loved and connected to God.

The greatest gift of Christ's sacrifice is restoring our direct connection with God. No longer needing intermediaries, there is no separation—only direct access to the divine presence that created and sustains us. This truth calls us to live differently, approaching each day with confidence that we walk with God beside us, within us, before us, and behind us.

When we realize there is no separation between us and our Creator, we begin to see others differently—not as separate from us, but as fellow travelers on the journey home.

How can you live as if the veil has genuinely been lifted for you, because it has?

Section 7

DIVINE RESILIENCE

Chapter 31
The Spirit of Power

"For God has not given us a spirit of fear, but of power and of love and of a sound mind." –2 Timothy 1:7

I have this verse engraved on reclaimed wood in my office. I have been working on my fear stories my entire life, even if others don't see it. I was too afraid to leave my career and start a business for many years before I finally hired a coach to help me. When I resigned, it was a moment of courage and faith greater than my fear, but it quickly faded, and I began to worry again about whether I had made the right decision.

When I left, I met an artist at a friend's house who works with recycled timber. I commissioned her to create a piece for me with this verse so I could see it every day, all day long. I don't remember the first time I read this verse, but when I reread it as I was leaving my corporate career and starting my own business, I clung to it for strength and encouragement. I felt like it was a promise that God made to me, a reminder of who I am.

Faith Over Fear

Paul wrote these words in a letter to Timothy, a young leader in the church. Timothy was feeling the burden of persecution, struggling with doubt, and even facing the fear of death that many Christians were experiencing. Paul's words served as a strong reminder that fear does not come from God. When we receive the Holy Spirit, we are given power, love, and self-discipline to face any situation.

This verse really resonates with me. When I started my business, I still felt a lot of fear. The pain of staying in my corporate job became greater than the fear of the unknown, so I left after twenty-two years. I waited for the moment when the scale would tip, and I acted quickly because I was so scared that if I hesitated, my courage would fade.

I've realized that I need consistent reinforcement to maintain my faith over fear. Surrounding myself with images and words that support my vision and remind me of God's promises helps keep me grounded during uncertain times. I need regular reminders that God has not given us a spirit of fear, that fear is the opposite of love, and that my God is the very embodiment of love itself.

Power, Love, and a Sound Mind

God tells us that our spirit is made of power, love, and a sound mind. I prefer the King James Version, which says, "sound mind" instead of "self-discipline" and "self-control," because a sound mind reminds me that God has given us discernment. That's what the Holy Spirit does. He gives us discernment, a sound mind, and intuition. If God says this is what my spirit is made of, who am I to argue? I choose to hold on to this reminder.

I wonder how many dreams were crushed by fear before they ever had a chance to come true. Fear is a short word, but it carries a lot of weight. Each of us has things we're afraid to do, and overcoming that fear is often where we find freedom, joy, adventure, confidence, and surprises.

I've learned that facing what scares us the most is usually what we should be running toward, not away from. We are born with only two fears: the fear of loud noises and the fear of falling. Those seem like valid fears to be hardwired with to protect ourselves from harm. The other fears we develop and learn over time. After years of conditioning, we become afraid of different things and instinctively seek comfort instead. Comfort feels good; it's easier and less frightening. But it doesn't make for a great adventure, nor does it light us up or feel exhilarating, and it doesn't foster growth. Comfort is where we should rest when needed, not the default state of our lives.

Overcoming Our Conditioning

From my own experiences, I know we can redefine success. I believe with all my heart that when we look within to find what truly brings us joy, then we can start creating and living a life we love.

It's not easy, and choosing to leap is probably the hardest part. The decision to make a change, despite our fears, reflects the courage of the human spirit. When the thought of not changing becomes more painful than the fear of the unknown, and the only option is to trust in our faith, that's when our stories become more powerful.

Living life on autopilot may be easier and more comfortable, but we can choose to live intentionally and change our jobs, careers, and relationships to create a life of greater alignment. It requires mindset shifts and perseverance to take daily action into unfamiliar territory, but we are so much stronger than we think we are.

My Fear Story

I've spent most of my life feeling afraid. I worried about being judged, wanted to be liked, fit in, and succeed. I also didn't want to disappoint anyone or upset my family, friends, community, or coworkers. I often second-guessed my decisions and choices, avoided taking risks, played it safe, and didn't want to draw attention to myself. I did many things in private because I was scared to be fully seen.

The most significant risk I took in my adult life was leaving the corporate career I knew to build a more aligned life and business for myself. People often ask how and why I made that move. How did I trade the comfort of a steady paycheck for the uncertainty of starting something new? I tell them I leaped when my faith grew bigger than my fear. I didn't have everything figured out, but I was more excited about figuring it out than about spending another fifteen years or so doing a job I no longer loved.

When you leave your job, your calendar clears. No meetings. No one else's agenda. Nobody is telling you when to wake up, what to do that day, or what to wear. Everything is completely open. The possibilities are endless and can feel overwhelming, like the sound of silence and the discomfort of stillness.

After I left, and it was just me and my little computer working alone, I had moments of panic. When I searched for the word "fear" in my daily journal that I've been keeping since I left my previous career, the word appeared in my search over 400 times.

I noticed doubts and negative thoughts creeping in again. I was still working through old patterns of worrying about security, stability, and comfort, which resurfaced. To combat these thoughts, I started repeating positive affirmations until I fell asleep, and it helped me get a restful night's sleep. I also began reading books about truth and watched a TED Talk by Tim Ferriss on facing our fears and using Stoicism as a philosophy to live better lives. I didn't know who Tim Ferriss was then, but his story inspired me because of how he handled his fearful thoughts.

Facing Our Fears

He created a template to list his fears, explore possible outcomes, develop plans to reduce risks, and then reassess the upside potential. What could happen? What would he give up if he stuck with the status quo? That change in perspective doesn't happen often enough. Our monkey brain spends so much time fixating on worst-case scenarios that it paralyzes us with fear and stops us from acting.

The interesting part is that if we logically analyze those fears, develop plans to reduce the perceived risk, and then focus on the benefits of executing those plans, we are much more likely to do the things that scare us most.

I did this exercise myself after watching the TED Talk; it was life-changing. The fear exercise revealed the dark, murky thoughts lurking beneath the surface—thoughts I didn't dare to speak aloud. The thoughts I felt ashamed of having. The fears of failure, disappointment, judgment, and embarrassment. Everything I worried about as a child persisted into adulthood. When I focused on "what if the opposite was true?" the story became so beautiful that I couldn't, and wouldn't, turn back.

Choosing to settle for the status quo means giving up the opportunity for a truly remarkable life. Settling involves relying on myself and trying to control everything around me. Stepping out in faith requires me to surrender control to God, allowing Him to guide my steps, align resources, and open doors to new opportunities. God always uses those who can't do it all on their own. He can use me, but as a gentleman, He waits for me to do my part and declare that I am ready. I'm ready.

I often revisit this exercise when I'm afraid to try something new. I can look back and see that none of my fears came true, and by choosing to act instead of letting my fears hold me back, I was able to grow and have incredible experiences.

I do this exercise with all my coaching clients. It's eye-opening to write down our fears on paper and then note what we would give up if we chose to stay afraid.

Here's how to do this exercise yourself:

1. Write down all your fears—put everything on paper.
2. Answer: "What if the complete opposite of this fear were true instead?"
3. What would that look like?
4. How can you reduce the risk related to this fear?
5. What would you be sacrificing if you chose to remain fearful and avoid taking action?

I hope this exercise uncovers some illogical thinking and encourages you to try some amazing new things instead! We have limited time here, and this world needs what you offer.

Your Power Practices

The exercises below are designed to help you recognize your fears, change your perspective, and embrace the power God has given you. Take your time with each one, allowing space for honest reflection and real change.

1. Journal Prompt

What have you discovered about your fears? Which fears are preventing you from moving forward? What might happen if you embraced your spirit of power, love, and sound mind? What is one practice that could help you build more courage in daily life?

2. Embodiment Exercise: Power Pose & Breathwork

Stand tall and place your hands on your hips or stretch your arms out wide.

Take three deep breaths. With each inhale, imagine breathing in strength, love, and clarity. With each exhale, let go of fear and doubt.

Speak the verse aloud: "God has not given me a spirit of fear, but of power, love, and a sound mind."

Hold this posture for one minute. Feel the change in your energy. Notice how your body responds to standing confidently.

The spirit of fear cripples us, making us smaller than we are meant to be. But remember, that spirit doesn't come from God. He has given you power to move mountains, love that can change relationships, and a sound mind to recognize the truth from lies.

When we choose to live guided by this divine spirit instead of fear, we embrace the fullness of who we are meant to be. Our lives grow, our impact deepens, and we discover abilities within ourselves that we never knew we had.

Your spirit of power is ready. Will you accept it today?

Chapter 32

The Value of Knowing Christ

"Yes, everything else is worthless when compared with the infinite value of knowing Christ Jesus my Lord. For his sake I have discarded everything else, counting it all as garbage, so that I could gain Christ" –Philippians 3:8

A few years ago, I was at my niece's wedding when a friend told me, "It was a gutsy move to give up everything." He was referring to me quitting my job, leaving behind a twenty-five-year corporate career along with a steady paycheck, bonuses, and other incentives that came with it. Without hesitation, I answered, "I gave up what I had in order to gain what I needed in my life." What I meant was something like Philippians 3:8.

Paul wrote this letter to the Philippians while he was in prison in Rome, awaiting trial. Can you imagine being as loving, hopeful, and faithful while in prison for your faith and not knowing what would happen to you? That's what was happening with Paul.

Paul was once a Pharisee named Saul who persecuted Christians. On his way to Damascus, he encountered the resurrected Jesus and was blinded by a bright light for three days. Later, a Christian named Ananias, whom God instructed to visit him, went to Saul. When Ananias laid hands on him, Saul's sight was restored. From that moment, he became Paul and grew to be one of the most influential figures in the early Church, and is believed to have written much of the New Testament.

Saul used to boast about his pedigree, background, accomplishments, education, and social status. But after meeting Christ, none of that mattered. He considered all those things as "worthless" compared to knowing Christ Jesus. He sacrificed everything, left his old life behind, and followed Jesus. His focus was on God, not himself.

Finding True Worth

I used to tie my worth to my achievements. Then, I let go of the idea that my job, title, salary, and everything that came with them defined my value. It didn't bring me happiness or fulfillment. I chased after success, hoping to finally find contentment and satisfaction, but that day never arrived. Instead, I felt more drained and anxious, and getting out of bed in the morning became harder.

Since leaving that old life behind, taking my leap of faith, honoring what is in my heart, releasing fear, trusting God, opening my hands and arms wide, and allowing myself to be a vessel for Him and His goodness, I have discovered a deep joy, a profound sense of purpose, and an inner knowing that my life matters, I am doing the right thing, and I am fully supported. I see any limitations only as the limits of my mind.

I used to think I had to plan every step before I allowed myself to dream. My dreams were limited by my ability to figure out how to make them happen. Then I realized that the dream and vision come first, and afterward, God provides the light and the way each day for the next best step.

A Journey of Faith

Journal Entry, August 25, 2021

I took myself on a solo date today. I wanted to leave my home office and go to an off-site spot to write, think, read, and strategize.

I change my environment when I become comfortable with my routine or need to grow. Stepping outside our comfort zones is a great way to spark new ideas, break free from conditioned responses, shift perspectives, and dream bigger.

Many restaurants are closed on Mondays, so it wasn't easy, but I eventually found my way back to Southside in Tremont. It's so beautiful here, and I'm dressed up for my date with myself. The weather is lovely, if the rain stays away. I am under an umbrella, so hopefully, that will help.

I found a beautiful patio spot at Southside, ordered a delicious meal, and alternated between listening to *The Power of Your Subconscious Mind* by Joseph Murphy and reading *Fearless* by Rebecca Minkoff.

Although quite different, both books emphasize the power of our subconscious mind to overcome limiting thoughts and beliefs. Through our thoughts, we can unlock creativity, strengthen relationships, shape the life we desire, and find true freedom.

Within a few minutes, the ideas started flowing, my energy increased, and I was ready to document what was happening.

In *The Power of the Subconscious Mind*, this book, along with others that focus on the subconscious mind, includes passages from the Bible, many attributed to Jesus. It's incredible how we can read or hear something multiple times, and each time, a new truth resonates.

I feel like the Church has guided me so far, and my exploration of comparative religions, yoga, meditation, and mysticism has brought me closer to God. I feel more connected to God and understand why it says we should pray fervently and endlessly, with faith and conviction that can move mountains.

Limitless Possibilities

As I reflect on my goals and current actions, I realize even greater potential to share these insights with my coaching clients, helping them expand their thinking and see the mind as fertile ground where seeds can be planted, nurtured, nourished, and patiently harvested. This morning, I practiced this meditation again, guiding everyone through a visualization of the garden. This time, the skies opened, and water and nourishment rained down onto the soil and seeds.

Repeatedly, God tells us, "By your faith, it shall be done." I no longer fear. I no longer believe I have to figure it out. I will not force or manipulate results. I will focus on aligning with God, deepen my faith even more, and keep affirming what I want to see manifest.

I am fully supported by God in every way as I help an unlimited number of people awaken and make transformational changes in their lives.

I am a vessel through which God carries out His plans for those He brings to me.

I am aligned and connected to God, so my business naturally grows exponentially.

I am a faithful wife, mother, daughter, sister, friend, and coach.

I am truly and honestly myself in all interactions.

I am a servant of God; therefore, God grants me financial and geographical freedom, along with other liberties from limitations to support me.

I am a world-renowned coach, author, speaker, creator, podcaster, and retreat planner, recognized for my expertise in guiding sustainable, transformational healing and change.

I am the proud owner and founder of a thriving and growing business.

I am a world traveler, explorer, and adventurer. I am fearless because God reminds me, "You have not been given a spirit of fear but of power, love, and sound mind."

I am at my ideal health—my mind, body, and spirit are all in harmony. I am at my natural, healthy weight.

I am strong, flexible, and optimally fit.

I make healthy choices for myself daily. I am joyful, kind, loving, compassionate, and live with an open heart.

I have big dreams and know that only God can make them come true. God told Moses that. Jesus repeated it often. Our job isn't to figure out how to do any of it. Our job is to step back and let God work through us so He can shine brightly and show others what's possible. That's letting go and surrendering. That's releasing control.

Your Christ-Centered Practices

As we explore what it truly means to value Christ above all else, let's put these principles into practice. The following exercises are designed to help you experience the freedom that comes with surrendering and reordering your priorities around knowing Christ.

1. Journal Prompt

What are the most important things you value in life? How would it feel to surrender and let God work through you effortlessly? What is one practice that could help you develop more Christ-centered priorities?

2. Embodiment Exercise: Letting Go, Gaining Christ

Sit or stand with your eyes closed. Either physically or mentally, hold an object in your hands that represents something you value deeply.

Close your eyes and reflect. How deeply do you genuinely value this in your heart?

Now, gently let it go. Picture it drifting up into the sky above. Open your hands and release the attachment.

Say aloud: "Knowing Christ is my greatest treasure. Everything else is secondary."

Breathe deeply and experience the freedom of releasing what does not serve your highest purpose.

When we realize the infinite value of knowing Christ, everything else—achievements, possessions, status, comfort—comes into proper perspective. Like Paul, we understand that what we once saw as gain is really loss compared to the surpassing greatness of knowing Jesus.

We view everything from a new perspective, with increased freedom. When Christ becomes our greatest treasure, paradoxically, we gain the life we were meant to have.

Your journey of surrender begins. Will you start valuing Christ above everything today?

Chapter 33
Overcoming the World

"I have told you these things, so that in me you may have peace. In this world you will have trouble. But take heart! I have overcome the world." –John 16:33

Jesus knew our journeys wouldn't be easy. They would be tough, sometimes painful, sometimes glorious, and we would experience all human emotions. Yet, He overcame the world. He rose above them all, and we can find peace in that.

As both fully divine and fully human, Jesus experienced all the emotions, feelings, desires, doubts, and fears we face. He wept, became angry, was brave, and cried out to His Father in heaven when He was scared. He loved, and He was loved deeply. He lived, and He knew His death would come unless God in heaven intervened.

When He spoke these words to the disciples, it was the night before He would be crucified. He told them that He would return to His Father in heaven, and they would be left without Him. He said they would face persecution, but the Holy Spirit would come to guide them after His death. He was preparing them for what was to come next.

I find it reassuring that Jesus wasn't trying to sugarcoat what was going to happen. He didn't say, "Just believe, and everything will be okay." He didn't tell them they wouldn't feel pain or difficulties. He acknowledged that they would. And then he said, "But take heart! I have overcome the world."

Taking heart means being brave, finding hope, and moving forward despite challenges. When Jesus says He has overcome the world, it means He has conquered evil, the struggles of this world, and the pain we experience.

The Spirit of Truth

A few verses later, Jesus tells His disciples about the Holy Spirit:

"I have much more to say to you, more than you can now bear. But when he, the Spirit of truth, comes, he will guide you into all the truth. He will not speak on his own; he will speak only what he hears, and he will tell you what is yet to come. He will glorify me because it is from me that he will receive what he will make known to you. All that belongs to the Father is mine. That is why I said the Spirit will receive from me what he will make known to you."

I don't know if the disciples truly understood what it meant that He would send the Spirit of truth to each of them. We have access to the Holy Spirit 24/7. For some reason, I've always known that the Holy Spirit lives within me. I know I can ask questions and get answers. I trust my gut and intuition, knowing the Spirit guides me to understand what is right and wrong. It's only when I don't listen or try to do things my own way that things don't go well.

While Jesus was alive, He played that role for the disciples, training them as we train children. Once He left them, we all received the Spirit instead. I don't remember hearing much about the Holy Spirit at church. The focus was more on the Father and Son than the Spirit.

Finding Peace in Trouble

Journal Entry, February 15, 2023

I woke up this morning feeling heavy-hearted. I'm anxious and worry about what the future holds. Some days, that burden feels overwhelming.

And then I remembered one of my favorite verses—the one where Jesus says, "In this world you will have trouble. But take heart! I have overcome the world." It hit me differently today. He doesn't promise we won't face troubles. In fact, He guarantees we will. But He also promises we can find peace in Him.

I reflected on this today. The promise isn't that the journey will be easy, but that we have an anchor to hold us through the storms. I can't control every outcome, but I can control where I focus my attention. When I focus on my worries, they seem even more overwhelming. When I focus on Jesus, on the Holy Spirit inside me, on God's promises, I find peace.

I realize I've spent too much time trying to avoid or quickly fix "troubles" instead of learning to find peace amid them. What if the troubles aren't just obstacles but opportunities to experience God's peace more deeply? What if, instead of praying for smooth waters, I learn to ride the waves?

Today, I choose to be courageous. Not because everything is perfect, but because I serve a God who has already conquered the world. I don't need to conquer it—He already has. I just need to stay connected to Him.

Already Overcome

The older I get, the more I understand this verse. My life hasn't been free of trouble, pain, disappointment, heartbreak, or loss. I've faced struggles, doubts, grief, pain, and fears. And, I have also known deep joy, profound love, incredible opportunities, and miraculous provision.

In my darkest moments, when I've felt most alone or afraid, the Holy Spirit has whispered reminders of God's presence and promises. Sometimes these come as gentle nudges toward scripture, other times through the words of a friend, and sometimes in the quiet of prayer. I now understand that peace isn't the absence of trouble but the presence of God in it.

When Jesus says He has "overcome the world," He isn't just talking about His victory over death, although that is a significant part of it. He's referring to His triumph over everything that separates us from God—fear, sin, doubt, pain, and even death itself. His overcoming means our problems are temporary, and His victory lasts forever.

I've learned to face challenges differently now. Not with the false idea that faith means an easy life, but with a deep understanding that no matter what happens, I am never alone. The same Spirit that raised Christ from the dead lives in me. The same God who parted the Red Sea guides my steps. The same love that went to the cross loves me unconditionally.

When challenges come—and they will—I think of these words and find strength. Not because I am strong, but because the one who lives in me has already overcome the world.

Your Peace Practices

The exercises below help you move from simply knowing about Christ's peace to truly experiencing it. Through reflection, embodied practice, and honest assessment, you'll begin to root yourself in the unshakable truth that no matter what challenges you face, you serve a God who has already overcome the world.

1. Journal Prompt

How do you find peace in tough times? Remember a moment when you felt God's presence during a difficult season. How did your faith help you?

2. Embodiment Exercise: Anchoring in Peace

Find a comfortable position and take a deep breath.

Imagine a stormy sea, symbolizing life's challenges. Feel the uncertainty and chaos.

Now, imagine Jesus standing on the water, reaching out His hand to you, just as He did with Peter.

Take another deep breath and say aloud: "In Christ, I have peace, for He has overcome the world."

Feel the shift in your body. Notice how peace replaces fear when you lean into His strength.

The peace Jesus provides isn't temporary—it's built on the unshakable truth that He has already overcome everything that tries to overwhelm us. This peace is available beyond our circumstances, and keeps us grounded when everything else feels unstable.

Peace isn't found in perfect circumstances but in complete trust in the One who holds all circumstances in His hands.

Your pathway to peace awaits. Will you take heart today?

Chapter 34

The One Thing That Matters

"'Martha, Martha,' the Lord answered, 'you are worried and upset about many things, but few things are needed—or indeed only one. Mary has chosen what is better, and it will not be taken away from her.'" –Luke 10:41–42

I enjoy reading passages where Jesus is with His friends. This lesson about the sisters Mary and Martha speaks directly to me because this is something I struggle with, and makes me laugh, reminding me of what's most important. Jesus was close to Lazarus and his two sisters, Mary and Martha. Jesus visited the sisters, and Martha was busy in the kitchen preparing for Jesus's arrival. She was probably cooking, cleaning, rushing around, trying to make everything perfect. But her sister Mary wasn't helping her. She sat at Jesus's feet and listened to Him teach.

I imagine Martha is the older sister and the more responsible one, although it's not explicitly stated. During this visit, Martha grew frustrated and asked Jesus to tell Mary to help her. Jesus reminded Martha—and me—that the only thing that truly matters is being fully present with Him. Mary did the right thing by listening, being present, and not leaving Jesus's side. Martha tried to earn favor through service and action, while Mary simply chose to be present.

Doing vs. Being

Although Martha was fulfilling her societal expectations for women at that time and even today in many households, Jesus used Mary as a better example. This lesson has become one of the most important in my life. I have spent most of my life focusing on doing, achieving, and operating with masculine energy. While that often brings success in the world, Jesus shows us that Mary exemplifies beautiful feminine energy.

Instead of trying to impress Jesus, Mary chose to honor Him. She was present, in the moment, listening actively and connecting deeply. This is what I return to every day. In quiet moments with God, I find peace. In these moments, I hear from Him. In these moments, I discover a love that is so deep. By simply being, I trust, listen, and find clarity.

Although I've read this story many times, it feels different today. It highlights the modern contrast between doing and being, busyness and presence. Hustle versus flow. What the world teaches and expects isn't what God is asking of us.

The Tyranny of Busyness

I've often wondered how Martha was feeling at that moment. Was she resentful? Overwhelmed? Maybe she truly believed that serving Jesus the perfect meal was the best way to show her love. Still, in her rush, she missed the presence of the very one she was trying to serve.

How many times have I fallen into the same pattern? Rushing through my morning devotions just to check them off my list before moving on to "more important" tasks. Planning events while missing the real purpose of gathering. Even using my spiritual gifts to serve others, all the while my own connection with God grows distant.

Our culture celebrates being busy. We showcase our full schedules like badges of honor. "How are you?" someone asks, and we reply, "Busy!" as if it's the highest compliment. We've been taught that our worth depends on our productivity, that sitting still is wasting time, and that listening is less important than doing.

But Jesus gently corrects this mindset. He doesn't scold Martha for her service—He addresses her worry and distraction. "Martha, Martha," He says with such tenderness I can almost hear His voice. "You are worried and upset about many things." Isn't that the truth about our busy lives? The more we do, the more worried and upset we become.

Finding Center Again

Journal Entry, July 10, 2022

I realized today that I've been Martha-ing my way through life again. I am so busy doing things for God that I haven't had time to simply be with God. My prayer life has become a rushed list of requests. My Bible reading has turned into another task to check off. Even my service at church feels mechanical rather than joyful.

This morning, I sat in silence for thirty minutes. No agenda, no requests, just being present with God. At first, my mind raced with all the things I should have been doing instead, but gradually, a peace settled over me that I hadn't felt in months. I heard no audible voice or received any dramatic revelation, but somehow, I knew I was exactly where I needed to be—at the feet of Jesus, doing the one thing that truly matters.

I'm recommitting to this practice every day, even if some tasks go unfinished, the house isn't perfect, and emails pile up. I'm prioritizing what's more important, and I won't let it be taken away from me.

How easy it is to slip back into Martha-mode. The world doesn't pause its demands just because we decide to focus on being with God. If anything, the pressure increases. There's always one more email to answer, one more task to complete, one more person to help. The challenge isn't finding time once; it's consistently choosing the better thing every day.

Learning to Sit at His Feet

What does it mean to be like Mary in today's world? It doesn't necessarily mean abandoning all responsibilities or never serving others. It means finding our center in Christ before reaching outward. It involves serving from abundance rather than obligation. It also means recognizing that our primary identity isn't based on what we do but on whose child we are.

Mary chose to sit at Jesus's feet—the traditional position of a disciple. She was not passive; she was actively learning, absorbing, and growing. Her posture revealed her priority: to know Jesus, not just serve Him.

This distinction changes everything. When we understand who we are in Christ—deeply loved, fully accepted, eternally valued—our actions come from a different place. We serve not to seek approval but because we already have it. We work not to prove our worth but because we already know it. We love not to receive love in return but because we're already filled with it.

Perhaps the most beautiful part of this story is Jesus's promise that what Mary has chosen "will not be taken away from her." In a world where everything feels temporary—health, relationships, achievements, possessions—this one thing remains eternal. Our connection with Jesus is the only thing that can never be lost, stolen, or destroyed. It's worth rearranging our entire lives to gain it.

Your Presence Practices

As we reflect on Jesus's gentle reminder that only one thing is truly needed, let's practice shifting from a Martha mindset of constant doing to a Mary posture of being present with Him. The following exercises encourage you to experience the transformative power of prioritizing presence over productivity. Through journaling, embodied practice, and honest assessment, you'll begin to discover what it means to choose 'what is better' in your own life—the one thing that truly matters and cannot be taken away.

1. Journal Prompt

Describe a moment when you felt a deep connection with God. What was that experience like? When do you feel most disconnected? Which activities or habits tend to pull you into "Martha mode," and how could you balance them with more "Mary moments"?

2. Embodiment Exercise: Resting in His Presence

Find a peaceful spot and sit comfortably.

Close your eyes and take a deep breath. Release the mental to-do list.

Picture yourself at Martha's house. Visualize Jesus sitting in the room.

Hear Him calling your name, gently inviting you to sit with Him.

Breathe in His peace and repeat this phrase: "I choose what is better. I rest in Your presence."

Stay in this posture for at least five minutes, simply being with Jesus without any agenda.

In our fast-paced world that values busyness and success, Jesus's words to Martha offer a powerful, counter-cultural invitation. The "one thing needed" isn't about doing more, impressing others, or even serving with good intentions. It's about choosing to be present with Him above all else.

This doesn't mean that practical service has no value—Martha's desire to serve was admirable. But when our actions become disconnected from being, and when our service is separated from relationship, we miss what matters most. Mary understood that being with Jesus wasn't just another priority—it was the priority that gives meaning to everything else.

When we understand this truth, everything changes. Our schedules reflect our priorities. Our stress levels decrease. Our service becomes more joyful and less prone to burnout. We become more attuned to God's voice and more responsive to His guidance. We realize that by focusing on the one essential thing, everything else naturally falls into place.

Your invitation to presence awaits. Will you choose what is better today?

Chapter 35

The Journey Home

"But while he was still a long way off, his father saw him and was filled with compassion for him; he ran to his son, threw his arms around him and kissed him." –Luke 15:20

The idea to include a chapter about the story of the prodigal son came to me in a dream. I woke up knowing that this was meant to be the final chapter. In my dream, God told me to remind everyone that they can always come home, not to condemnation or judgment, but to love and compassion. God is waiting for each of us to come back home to Him.

If you've never heard of the prodigal son, the story begins with a young man who asks for his inheritance early from his father and then leaves home to squander it. When he's lost, hungry, and broken, he ends up feeding pigs—a disgrace for a Jewish man. In his darkest moment, he decides that it's time to go back home.

He prepares his apology to his father: "Father, I have sinned against heaven and against you. I am no longer worthy to be called your son; make me like one of your hired servants."

He doesn't expect forgiveness from his father but hopes to be a servant in his house. Meanwhile, while he has been away, his father has watched the road every day, waiting for his son to come back. One day, he sees his son approaching home, and he is so overwhelmed that he runs to him, embraces him, and kisses him.

Before the son can even finish his rehearsed apology speech, the father calls for the best robe, a ring for his finger, sandals for his feet, and orders a feast to celebrate. "This son of mine was dead and is alive again; he was lost and is found."

When the older brother returns from working in the fields and hears the celebration, he becomes angry. He didn't want to go to the party and yelled at

261

his father: "Look! All these years, I've been slaving for you and never disobeyed your orders. Yet you never gave me even a young goat so I could celebrate with my friends. But when this son of yours, who has squandered your property with prostitutes, comes home, you kill the fattened calf for him!"

The father says, "My son, you are always with me, and everything I have is yours. But we had to celebrate and be glad because this brother of yours was dead and is alive again; he was lost and is found."

Living as Both Brothers

If I'm honest, I've lived like both brothers in the story of the prodigal son. The one who stays home and does what's expected, and the one who wanders, and then comes home hoping for redemption.

There were times when I was the older brother—obedient, dedicated, trying to be good, meet expectations, and do all the "right" things. I judged my worth based on how well I performed, how perfect I was, and the external praise I received from others. I believed that if I kept showing up and worked hard enough, I would finally feel seen. Then, I'd finally feel whole and valuable.

But instead of fulfillment, I felt fatigue and burnout. Instead of joy, I experienced pressure and numbness. Instead of deep peace, I sensed a growing ache and emptiness that nothing could fill.

And then there were the seasons when I was the younger brother.

I wandered—not always in dramatic ways, but subtly. I focused more on worldly experiences than spiritual alignment. I searched for deeper meaning, neglected my spiritual practices, and didn't stay in constant communion with God. I wanted to feel enough and truly alive.

Sometimes, it worked—for a little while. That brief feeling of satisfaction, the rush from doing, but then the silence would return. And with it, the realization that I'd strayed far from home. Not just from the things that matter, but from the One who gave me life. My values. My center. My peace.

The Father Who Waits and Watches

What I haven't considered before is the father's waiting. He doesn't try to find his son or send messages for his return. He doesn't cut him off or disown him. Instead, he respects his son's freedom while patiently waiting for his return. This is radical love—respecting our free will while eagerly waiting for reconciliation.

Now that I'm a parent, when I think about the father seeing his son and rushing to him, I can't help but cry. Without hesitation, explanation, or waiting for an apology, he runs toward his son.

This is our God, who runs to meet us before we even finish our rehearsed apologies. Our God, who restores us as His children when we expect to be servants, celebrates our return even when we don't think we deserve it.

The Spiritual Wandering

Looking back, my spiritual wandering wasn't just about running from God; it was about searching for something I didn't realize I already had.

I sought a spiritual connection beyond God and explored different paths, searching for something more profound and meaningful.

I read books and listened to podcasts about philosophies and practices that promised peace, healing, and power. But none of them could match the depth of love, truth, and transformation I've experienced in God's presence.

I followed my feelings instead of faith.

I trusted how I felt more than what God had said. If it felt good or expansive, I assumed it must be true. But feelings can be misleading and can change. They're powerful, but they're not the same as wisdom. Faith calls us to trust even when we don't feel it.

I tried to manifest my own peace.

I set intentions, visualized, and tried to manifest my way into purpose, passion, and peace. However, in all my efforts to create a life I loved, I forgot to ask my Creator what He had in mind for me.

I chose control instead of communion.

I was making plans instead of seeking presence. I wanted to control the outcome rather than surrender to God's wisdom. Then I remembered that communion and intimacy with God are what I was created for. It's what we're all created for.

I created my identity through effort.

I forgot that I was already loved, already His, and already enough just as I was. I didn't have to earn God's love; it was already mine. I was always His beloved daughter.

I believed I needed to heal myself.

I read the books, took the courses, did the work, and although my mind was filled with new knowledge, my heart and soul still longed for more. Only God's love could fill that emptiness.

When I Finally Turned Around

Coming home wasn't a dramatic breakdown for me; it was more like a quiet awakening. In silent moments, I heard God whisper, *"You don't have to keep running."*

I turned toward Him. I began reading His Word again and dedicated more time to gratitude and prayer. I took long walks alone in nature, sat, talked, and listened. What I found was not judgment but compassion. Just like the father in the story, God ran to meet me, opened His arms, and wrapped me in what I needed—His grace and unconditional love.

It undid me. It healed me.

Because, despite all the goals I'd set, the milestones I'd reached, and the dreams I'd chased, what I was truly searching for was already mine.

The purpose.

The passion.

The peace.

They were waiting in God's loving presence.

God's Arms Are Always Open

Here's what I want you to understand as you finish the last pages of this book:

You can always come home, whether you've been faithful or wandering, whether you've stayed or strayed, whether you're thriving or tired.

God isn't keeping score; He's patiently waiting and watching the road for you. And the moment you turn your heart toward Him, He runs—not with judgment, but with joy.

You are not too far gone. You are not too much. You are not too late.

You are *loved*. You are *His*. You are *home*.

Coming Home Practices

This isn't just a story to *understand*; it's one to *feel* deeply. I invite you to personalize this powerful story of homecoming. The reflections and embodied practice serve as an invitation to experience the loving embrace of the Father who watches and waits for you. Through journaling and a guided visualization, you'll be able to sense what it means to be welcomed home— not with judgment, but with joy and celebration. This isn't just about understanding grace mentally; it's about experiencing it deeply in your body and spirit.

1. Journal Prompts:
   - When have you felt like the older brother, doing what's expected but still feeling invisible?
   - When have you been the prodigal son—pursuing external things and ending up feeling empty?
   - What does "coming home" mean for you right now?
   - What does it mean to allow God to love you just as you are?

2. Embodiment Practice: Coming Home to Yourself and to God

Find stillness.

Sit or stand in a comfortable position. Rest your hands on your heart or your belly and close your eyes if that feels safe.

Take a couple of deep breaths.

Visualize the road.

Imagine yourself walking along a long path. You might feel tired, unsure, or even ashamed. But in the distance, you see someone running toward you. It's God. His arms are open, and His face is full of joy.

Step into the embrace.

Feel His arms around you. His voice whispering, *"Welcome home, my child."* Allow yourself to feel the safety, relief, and grace. Let your shoulders relax. Let your heart soften. Let God hold you.

Repeat this truth:

"I am home. I am loved. I am safe. I belong."

Rest.

Stay in this sacred space as long as you need. When you're ready, gently open your eyes. Breathe in the feeling of grace. Remember that this moment, this sensation, this sense of home, you can return to it again and again.

You don't have to earn God's love; you just need to *return*.

You can always come home.

Conclusion
The Light Has Always Been with You

This book was a divine assignment I didn't think I was ready for, was terrified to undertake, and it's been the gift of a lifetime because in the co-creation with God, my faith deepened. I faithfully said His name, I surrendered my doubt, I trusted that He would support me.

God pursued me, meeting me in that trembling, obedient "yes," and through every early morning writing session, each verse, reflection, and chapter, He revealed Himself to me again and again. This book is as much for me as it is for you.

What I realized while writing this book, re-reading my journal entries, and what I hope you've felt is that we are never truly alone. During my darkest days, my deepest doubts, and my greatest fears, He was with me the whole time. Any distance I felt was because I created it, not because God moved away. I was reminded of the times my faith wavered, the times it was strong, and throughout it all, of God's faithfulness and promises.

If there's any distance between you and God, the way back home isn't far away. It is available to each of us right here, right now. The lanterns to light our path, answers, clarity, unconditional love, and peace we seek are accessible when we reach out and connect with God.

How amazing that words written thousands of years ago still speak to our struggles and point us back to our loving Creator who knows us and loves us unconditionally.

As I've shared chapters of this book with early readers, I was humbled by their stories of religious trauma, deep wounds, and years of wandering, while seeking a connection to something greater. Their words about how the chapters have rekindled their faith have been humbling and overwhelming. Not by anything I've done, except stepping aside for God to work through me.

My prayer is that each verse serves as a lantern, illuminated by Him, for you.

What I Want You To Remember

May each verse and story be a reminder that:

Your faith is still alive.

Your journey doesn't end here.

Surrender is strength.

Your purpose is real.

Provision is already on the way.

Transformation is possible.

Love is the foundation.

And joy and peace are your inheritance as a child of God.

You may have forgotten, gotten lost, or pulled away. But He never did.

He has always been here waiting. He still is, right now.

And so, if you remember only one thing, let it be this:

You can always come home.

Back to the truth of who you are and whose you are.

Back to a love that does not falter.

Back to the light that has been within you all along.

This book was my offering to Him and you. A divine assignment I once resisted but now release with gratitude. I wrote it in the darkness of early mornings and in the light. I wrestled with God, surrendered, wept, and worshipped. And in that sacred process, I found my way home, too.

If these lanterns of light have lit even one step of your path, I am so grateful.

May you keep walking.

Keep trusting.

Keep showing up with your whole heart.

There is more ahead. And you are never alone.

The lanterns are yours now. Let them guide you home, again and again.

Welcome home.

Continue Your Journey with
Lanterns of Light™

Your journey doesn't end here with the final chapter; this is just the beginning. I'd love to stay connected with you and welcome you into my community. I've created additional resources to help you go deeper, embody the practices, and support you on your faith journey.

As an avid reader, I've found that when I apply the lessons and complete the exercises, I don't just learn new information—I experience transformation. Whether you use the resources on your own, as part of a book club, or with a Bible study, may they meet you exactly where you are.

Scan the QR code below (or visit www.LanternsOfLight.com/bonus) to access:

- Guided journal prompts for each chapter
- Recordings of embodiment practices
- Mini video episodes where I share reflections on each chapter
- An invitation to join my private newsletter community

May your path be illuminated and serve as a reminder of who you are, whose beloved child you are, and what you are here to create. Shine brightly, and step forward knowing you are guided, supported, and loved unconditionally.

With gratitude,

Aneta

Thank You

Two small words that don't seem to be enough for the amount of gratitude in my heart. This book would not exist without the countless people in my life who have loved me, encouraged me, and believed in me all along.

To Dorel, Isabella, and Alexandra – I don't have words to express what you mean to me. The greatest blessing of my life is that God brought us all together as a family. I can't imagine doing life with anyone else. You believed that I could write this book when I was too scared to begin. You read chapters and drafts and listened patiently throughout the entire process. Thank you for always being my biggest supporters. I love you.

To George – my editor and friend, who has seen every version of this book. Thank you for saying "yes" again, for your encouragement when I hesitated, for your kindness when I was scared, and for making my work better with each revision. I can't imagine creating this without you.

To my many early readers – your willingness to read early drafts and share your feedback gave me the courage to keep going. You know who you are, and your words now live without these pages. I am forever grateful.

To my sister Elizabeth, my parents, grandparents, and great-grandparents – thank you for being examples of faith. Throughout your lives, I have witnessed what it means to be in the Word, to experience doubt, struggle, and question, and most importantly, to have faith that endures all circumstances.

To my grandmother Ana – she was the first person to open a Bible to me. I remember watching you read your Bible daily, and when I visited, we'd read together, and you asked me what I thought the passages meant. As a young child, I didn't realize that you were giving me a lifelong gift of knowing that the Holy Spirit dwells within me, guides me, and gives me spiritual eyes to see and ears to hear. I hope you're smiling down on me now.

And most importantly, to God – my Creator, the source of all that is. Thank you for entrusting me with this assignment, for the privilege of co-creating with You, and for loving me unconditionally throughout my life's journey. I don't know if this is what You expected when You chose me, but I hope I have made You proud.

Finally, to you, the reader – thank you for picking up this book and allowing this book to be a part of your own journey. My prayer is that these words are lamps to your feet, that you have faith the size of a mustard seed, and that you always remember that you can come home to your loving God. May your path always be lit.

With deep gratitude,

Aneta

About the Author

Aneta Ardelian Kuzma is the Founder and CEO of the Ardelian Kuzma Group, a transformational coach, speaker, and wellness consultant dedicated to helping people live the width of their lives and create lives of purpose, passion, and peace. She helps professionals and organizations move from burnout to alignment and lead with clarity and confidence.

After more than twenty-five years in the corporate world, Aneta experienced firsthand the toll of overachievement and burnout. Her own journey of redefining success, finding alignment, and creating sustainable practices inspired her to launch her coaching and consulting practice in 2019.

Through her books, podcast, programs, and retreats, Aneta equips people worldwide to release what no longer serves them, reconnect with their true selves, and design lives anchored in peace and purpose.

She is the author of *Live the Width of Your Life*™, host of the *Live the Width of Your Life*™ *Podcast,* and leads transformational retreats around the world.

Her mission is to help others remember that they are enough—and that we are created to live the width, not just the length, of our lives. You can learn more about her programs, wellness sessions, and retreats, or sign up for her newsletter at: www.anetakuzma.com.